LEADE

IN HEALTHCARE

Values at the Top

LEADERSHIP IN HEALTHCARE

Values at the Top

Carson F. Dye

Health Administration Press

04   03   02   01   00   5   4   3   2   1

Library of Congress Cataloging-in-Publication Data

Dye, Carson F.
    Leadership in healthcare: values at the top/Carson F. Dye.
       p.   cm. — (ACHE management series)
    Includes bibliographical references.
    ISBN 1-56793-114-6 (alk. paper)
    Health services administration. 2. Leadership
    I. Title: Leadership in health care II. Title.
    III. Management series (Chicago, IL).
    RA971.D937 2000
    362. 1'068'4—dc21

                                                  99-047342
                                                    CIP

The paper used in this publication meets the minimum requirements of American National Standards for Information Sciences—Permanence of Paper for Printed Library Materials, ANSI Z39.48–1984. ♾ ™

Health Administration Press
A division of the Foundation of the
   American College of Healthcare Executives
One North Franklin Street, Suite 1700
Chicago, IL 60606-3491
312/424-2800

To my family—
Joaquina, Carly, Emily,
Liesl, and Blakely.

They have always shown
their faith in my work
and me and done so
with great
love and respect.

CONTENTS

Acknowledgments

THE WRITING OF ANY BOOK is a journey and any journey of any length requires help from others along the way. I cannot begin to list the many leaders I have observed over the years who have taught me the importance of values in leadership. Many did so without even knowing it. Working in the organizations I was privileged to serve allowed me to live in a learning laboratory. My years of teaching for the American College of Healthcare Executives has exposed me to many fine leaders and I have learned much from their examples and stories. Seminar leaders always learn so much from their audiences. My consulting work has also taken me into several very fine organizations providing me with even more opportunities to see effective leadership on the front lines. To those for whom I have been counted worthy of serving and counseling, I thank you for your model and examples. I have also been blessed over the years with some wonderful students in courses I taught at Ohio State, Xavier, and the University of Cincinnati. The questions they posed to me as their teacher helped me grow. Therefore, I address you, the readers, as a student of leadership, not a teacher.

I continue to be grateful for the early personal impact on me of leaders such as Tom Ruthemeyer, Sister Mary George, Mark Hanahan, Mike Gilligan, the late Ed Arlinghaus, Donald A. Cramp, and the late Dr. Lonnie Wright. Close colleagues and clients who exhibited great leadership values included Jim Kaskie, Kam Sigafoos, Edsel Cotter, Dave Purcell, Bob Sholis, Brad Neet, Otis Wilson, Dr. Dick Hartman, Gene Miyamoto, and Bob Coons. I am also appreciative of several special individuals who have worked with me over the years including Dr. Ed Pike, Dr. Greg Taylor, Carol Cogossi, Randy Schimmoeller, Gretchen Patton, Dave Squire, Walter McLarty, Brandon Melton, Earl McLane, Sy Sokatch, Terry Wilk, Paul Palmisano, Cliff Lehman, Bob Gesing, and Barry Cesafsky. These leaders have strong values and live and work by them. I have enjoyed watching the leadership style of several CEOs including Bill Ruse, Sister Nancy Linenkugel, Steve Mickus, Ed Curtis, Susan Hunsaker, Bill Kessler, John Carlisle, Otis Wilson, and countless others whom I hope are not offended by my oversight. I have appreciated the chance to work more closely with Mark Elliott, who is one of those "natural born leaders" described in this book. All of these individuals embody the message of this book in that each of them has shown me how powerfully values can drive leadership. They are worthy examples and are good role models for anyone looking for effective leadership.

I would like to express my appreciation to the many candidates that I have worked with on various search assignments who give me live samples of effective leadership in action. Several individuals took the time to review the original manuscript including Sister Nancy Linenkugel, Brad Higgins, Bill Ruse,

Mike Covert, Kam Sigafoos, and Dr. Lee Hammerling. I appreciate their insight and thoughts and, of course, their time.

I am also particularly appreciative of Rob Fromberg of Health Administration Press. His positive nature and support are great examples that many leaders should follow. His willingness to just be there to "kick around an idea" and his responsiveness are certainly driven by a strong and appropriate values system. I would be remiss to not save special mention to Jane Williams, my editor at Health Administration Press. Jane was absolutely superb in her help with my ideas and expressions. She is the consummate editor, getting very involved with my vision and actively supporting the directions I wanted to go. This book is much better because of her wonderful help.

And last but not least, writers do not write without support from the homefront. Throughout my career my family has always been supportive. My four daughters—Carly, Emily, Liesl, and Blakely—are sources of joy, comfort, and inspiration. They tolerate me when I steal moments from them to think and write. My wife Joaquina, is an editor, a supporter, a very classy lady, a great friend, and truly a champion. She has always been there for me and has always been a helpful critic of my writing and my ideas. I owe so much to these five women who share a life and a home with me.

Preface

I HAVE ALWAYS BEEN FASCINATED by leadership. As I began my career, I often wondered how some leaders inspired others to follow them with great passion while other leaders seemed to get no response from their followers. What was leadership? Was it a skill that people were born with or was it something that could be learned? Why were some leaders more effective than others? I also asked: How can I improve my own leadership skills?

Although I continue to observe and learn more, I have reached the following conclusions about leadership. Some leaders possess and live by deep, unwavering values that guide their personal and professional behavior and thought. Whether these values are inherent or learned early in life, those leaders who abide by these constructs have a natural ability to interact with and lead others effortlessly. These individuals are often referred to as "born" leaders. People who are not born leaders are not doomed to failure, however, because the values of these so-called born leaders may also be present in them but these values may be latent and need to be coaxed out. Becoming aware of the need for learning and practicing a sensitive, practical, and appropriate value system is the first step toward becoming a world-class leader.

OBSERVATIONS

I have worked in the healthcare field for almost thirty years in various capacities. My experiences as both a consultant and a hospital executive have enabled me to observe firsthand how leadership is defined, developed, and executed in healthcare organizations. The more I have observed, the more I have become aware of five interrelated issues that plague today's healthcare organizations and their leaders.

1. Leadership is difficult to define. The longer I study leadership, the more I realize that, although the results of effective leadership are so visible, the harder it becomes to precisely define what it is that produced those effective results. Although new "definitive" leadership books appear in bookstores almost every month, their themes seem to miss the mark by not fully delineating the underlying factors that affect the usefulness of leaders and their decisions. Most of these books present overly simplistic formulas or new ideas that function as the current "leadership du jour." Ideal exceptions, however, are books, such as those by Stephen Covey, that discuss the importance of understanding the deeper and more subjective aspects of leadership, particularly the values of effective leaders.

2. The healthcare industry does not have enough highly effective leaders. My personal experiences indicate that the number of effective leaders in all industries and fields has declined. The need in healthcare may be particularly acute, which concerns me deeply. My hope is that readers of this book will agree and will work together to enhance leadership effectiveness.

3. The healthcare industry is facing serious crisis and significant challenges. I often hear "This industry is a mess!" or "What a frustrating field we work in!" Comments such as these indicate the frustrations and uneasy feelings of many healthcare leaders today as they face the rapid transformation of the industry. They have grave concerns and many are leaving the field as a result. They are weary of the constant changes that they have experienced. They are tired. They have lost their spirit. And they have no hope for the future.

4. Leadership development is not a top priority for many senior executives. Although many executives, especially senior leaders, express an interest in leadership development, very little time and financial resources are actually devoted to it. This paradox is apparent when leadership development and travel become the first expenses to get cut when organizational budgets become tight. Senior executives have become so busy that they rarely take as much time as they once did to study leadership.

5. Highly effective leaders are almost always very values-driven. The concept of values, especially in leadership, is sometimes too ambiguous and too subjective for many leaders. Those who rely only on hard data and measurable standards often say that because values cannot be measured, they are too vague to describe and therefore not that applicable to leadership process. However, my observation of and conversations with highly effective leaders reveal and prove that following a value system is a major, consistent contributor to their success.

CHAPTER OVERVIEW

In the foreword, Fred Brown, former president and CEO of one of the pioneering and largest integrated delivery systems in the country, BJC Health System, reminds us of two important things:

(1) all of us in healthcare need to win back the public's trust, work together to do so, and do it quickly; and (2) healthcare leaders must remember and perform their "covenant" to the community and the public.

Part I—Leadership in Healthcare—contains Chapters 1 through 3 and stages the present condition that defines and plagues the industry and its leaders. Chapter 1—The Leadership Imperative—is a call to action in that it contends that we need effective leaders now more than ever because the industry is in a state of flux and demands leaders who can adapt to current and future changes. The chapter enumerates the problems that brought about the mandate and offers solutions to repair them. Chapter 2—The Values-Based Definition—summarizes some of the various definitions of leadership proposed in popular literature and introduces the thesis of this book—the significance of values-based leadership and its effect on overall organizational outcomes. Chapter 3—The Senior Leader Predicament—explores the contribution of senior leaders to both the problem of and the solution to inefficient operations. The chapter also introduces organizational factors that impede senior leaders.

Part II—Personal Values—contains Chapters 4 through 10 and catalogs the key values that dictate the leader's behavior and thought process. Chapter 4—Respect and Stewardship— reiterates that respect for self and others is one of the sure paths to better stewardship. Suggestions on how to give and earn respect as a steward are detailed. Chapter 5—Ethics and Integrity—espouses the virtue of being true to yourself and others. Chapter 6—Interpersonal Connection—introduces the significance of possessing "people skills" and argues that interacting with others is the key to earning support and trust. Chapter 7— Servant Leadership—extols the ideal principle of leadership: to serve others so they can better serve the organization. Chapter 8—Initiative to Make Change—characterizes the "change makers," who are the courageous leaders who seek, or are not

afraid of, alternative ways to improve conditions. Chapter 9—
Commitment—discusses the work ethics of leaders and their
resolve to get things done. Chapter 10—Emotional Intelligence—defines emotional maturity and energy, which are the
two components of emotional intelligence.

Part III—Team Values—contains Chapters 11 through 14 and
presents the values that hold a team intact and make it more
effective. Chapter 11—Cooperation and Sharing—emphasizes
the importance of each team member's contribution in meeting and decision making. Chapter 12—Cohesiveness and Collaboration—explains the "entrepreneurial spirit" and its role
in rallying the team to support the same goal. Chapter 13—
Trust—argues that trust is the first value that team members
must learn to give and expect to be able to cooperate with each
other. Chapter 14—Conflict Management—defends the existence of conflict within teams. The chapter contends that conflict
is beneficial for the team because without it the team becomes
complacent.

Part IV—Evaluation—contains Chapters 15 through 17 and
Appendices A through C. Each chapter and appendix offers
you—as a present or future leader and team member—a chance
to evaluate the performance of yourself, your team, and your
team members. Chapter 18—Measuring Leader Values and
Effectiveness—is written by industrial psychologist Jared Lock.
The chapter supports the theories within this book with empirical published data.

A section in most chapters called "Operationalize the Concept" defines each component of the chapter's subject matter
and offers specific suggestions on how to apply each and all in
real-world scenarios. The reappearance of some of these elements in certain chapters is intended to emphasize their significance. Self-evaluation questions that broach the main issues of
each chapter can be found at the end of each chapter. Quota-
tions from various healthcare leaders and observers are peppered
within the text, as well.

LESSONS

I hope that this book communicates three important messages:

(1) This is an exciting time for leaders—your leadership is truly needed.
(2) Leadership can be learned.
(3) Learn and develop a good value system because doing so will enhance your effectiveness as a person, a leader, and team member.

I hope that both practitioners and academics pay close attention to the research, discussed in Chapter 18, that gives credence to the correlation between having values and being effective, and I hope this subsequently starts an intense dialogue. I hope academics heed these values-based approaches and teach them to their students because the industry needs new leaders who are not only technically skilled but also emotionally mature.

Because some of the scenarios presented here were adopted from actual situations, you may recognize them and even have your own opinions about resolving them based on your own experience. As a result, you may disagree and find discomfort with some of the suggestions given. But keep an open mind because everyone—even the experts—always can benefit from knowing more and knowing differently. Although this book is not intended to be a complete treatise on leadership—much more could be written on the subject—it does intend to jump start you to reflect on your own values and how they affect you and those around you. In some respects, I am asking you to develop, articulate, and live by a credo, as this quote suggests:

When you clarify the principles that will govern your life and the ends that you will seek, you give purpose to your daily decisions. A personal creed gives you a point of reference for navigating the sometimes stormy seas of organizational life. Without a set of such beliefs, your life has no rudder, and you are easily blown about by the winds of fashion. A credo to guide you prevents confusion on the journey.

James Kouzes and Barry Posner[1]

Carson F. Dye
August 1999

Foreword

by Fred L. Brown, FACHE

LET'S FACE IT, THE WORLD of healthcare has been turned upside down. The last decade of the twentieth century has turned the word "healthcare" from a noun associated with maintenance of an individual's well-being to a modifier of words such as "costs," "crisis," or "reform," or some indicator of the aggregate debate. Thus, while patients received better care than at any other time in history, the healthcare industry remains under intense scrutiny. Focus group after focus group tells the same story—Americans have doubts. They don't trust healthcare anymore. They don't believe they have choices. They don't believe they have voices. They don't believe anyone listens to them anymore. If perception is indeed reality, then they are right.

As American healthcare prepares for a new millennium, healthcare leaders must play an important role in regaining America's trust. America's healthcare leaders are being asked to advance the debate beyond the business side of today's turbulent and complex healthcare organizations. Like no other time in history, healthcare must demonstrate its leadership role. To achieve this, healthcare leaders must turn to their most trusted and sage advisor—themselves. They must once again trust their own basic instincts, their own gut reactions. Reactions that are not based merely on business decisions, but based rather on doing what's right for our patients and communities.

Here's my advice to all healthcare leaders who feel they have lost their way: Let's keep it simple. Let's stay focused. We must—we have to—band together and renew our sacred covenant with our patients and communities. Since Ben Franklin founded the first American hospital, we have been the guardians of this silent covenant. If we need to rebuild public trust and return to values-based leadership, what better way to do it than by renewing this covenant? A covenant that calls on all of us to be there, to take care and give care in what we do, to open our doors and our hearts, and to extend our hands to our neighbors in good times and in bad. While we are keenly aware of our social obligations as healthcare providers, we must remind ourselves of the trust that the public bestowed upon us. A trust we see diminishing before our eyes. We must work together, as never before, to strike a greater balance between our public and private sector organizations that have a vested interest in creating healthier communities.

Let's begin with reminding ourselves why we chose this profession. Do you remember what ideals and emotions led you to give your time and talent to healthcare? All of us in healthcare have a special story to tell; my story may be very similar to yours. When I was growing up in Dunbar, West Virginia, I was greatly influenced by the values instilled in me by my parents. Over the years, I witnessed my father as an active community volunteer who supported little league teams and the Boy Scouts. My mother was a nurse. Together, their energy for life and community service inspired me and my sister to go into healthcare and sustained us on our journey.

Through my 35-year career, I have worked hard to live up to the values given to me by my family. In fact, I have developed my own personal mission statement to help keep me grounded; see a copy below. I carry a copy of it in my wallet so that I am reminded every day of what drives me and keeps me focused.

My mission is to:

- Serve my fellow man.
- Make my part of the world a better place for having been there.
- Bring out the best in others.

I will attempt to:

- Exemplify Christian values in all I do.
- Be a coach that teaches and motivates positively.
- Celebrate the successes of myself and others.
- Give more than I take from society, my organization, my family, and those with whom I interact.
- Continually learn about my work and the world around me.
- Seek balance between my quest to serve others and take time for my own enjoyment and personal relationships.

Ultimately, our collective stories, talent, and wisdom are what will guide us. I have always said that healthcare people are special—we got into this field because we care. However, our greatest strength is also our greatest fault. We, as a national community of caregivers, tend to carry our burdens alone. We want to be all things to all people, but it can't be done.

Although we carry a mantle of leadership in the communities we serve, we do not own the title of problem solver. We need to remember that we must reach out to all corners of our communities to look for more balanced approaches that can make each community healthier. This is the only path to a stronger American healthcare. But where does this balance come from? It comes from a sense of shared responsibility. Collaboration is the driving force behind healthcare leadership in the new century. A new century that must come to grips with our nation's lack of clear and direct social policy on healthcare.

The United States must find ways to improve the way it delivers and administers healthcare. The mandate to make healthcare responsible will be complex and rooted in a variety of social, political, economic, and technological factors. Healthcare providers, insurers, national and local governments, community groups, and patients must—and have to—work together to set a new course for socially responsible healthcare. How can healthcare leaders prepare themselves for this daunting challenge? I suggest we return to the basics—our values.

Leadership in Healthcare: Values at the Top is a refresher course on evaluating our personal and professional guiding principles. In a nutshell, it reinforces my belief that if we make decisions based simply on what's right and wrong, then we will weather any storm we encounter. In his book, Carson Dye offers sound and practical advice on how leaders can enhance their effectiveness by identifying, emphasizing, and applying certain core values. He also expands on many of the points that I brought up in this foreword including collaborating with others to produce mutually beneficial results and creating a personal mission statement.

Over the past decade, the resurgence of interest in healthy communities has drastically moved us back to thinking about our social responsibility—our covenant. Much continues to be written about corporate citizenship and mission fulfillment. But more often than we care to realize, or admit, we struggle with daily problems and business matters that distract us from our covenant and our values-based leadership roles. Sadly, market forces and economic reality have forced us to devote our attentions to market share, strategic plans, labor issues, and other matters important to survival. However, this focus creates a perception that we are too business-focused, rather than values-focused. This perception matters to our employees, patients, and communities. Now, common sense tells us that a financially strong institution is in a better position to fulfill our covenant than a weak one. No question about it. What the discussion comes down to is what many term "corporate soul." If we are making the necessary and tough business decisions today to protect our ability to live our mission tomorrow, then we can rest assured the short-term pain is worth the long-term gain. But these decisions cannot be done in a vacuum, especially decisions void of values and ethics. As we grapple with our own issues and leadership dilemmas, we must continue to serve as chief administrators, chief educators, chief motivators, and chief communicators. Yes, it is a challenge. Like most challenges, however, it is also a tremendous opportunity to demonstrate leadership.

I hope all healthcare leaders who read this book arrive at their own conclusions on how to make their communities better and healthier. In fact, this book serves a valuable function by reminding us of the importance of values in leadership and teaching us how to make ourselves more comfortable with our own leadership skills. Whether you're a nurse, physician, board member, volunteer, or other caregiver, you must remember that we are in healthcare to care for our patients and our communities. Don't let anyone tell you any differently. We will succeed by following our own values. We fail ourselves, and others, when we forget and lose sight of these values. This book offers a valuable reminder of our covenant obligations.

PART I

Leadership in Healthcare

Chapter One

THE LEADERSHIP IMPERATIVE

By any objective measure, the amount of significant, often traumatic, change in organization has grown tremendously over the past two decades. Powerful macroeconomic forces are at work here, and these forces may grow even stronger over the next few decades. As a result, more and more organizations will be pushed to reduce costs, improve the quality of products and services, locate new opportunities for growth, and increase productivity.

John Kotter[1]

ANOTHER BOOK ON LEADERSHIP? Enough already! Why do I need another to stack on top of the other half-way-read ones that clutter my desk and line my bookshelves? Why do I have to learn new tricks now? The answer to these laments is a simple syllogism: the healthcare industry is constantly evolving; you, as a leader, are part of the healthcare industry; therefore, you must constantly evolve, as well.

Evolution is a necessary evil. The evolution of healthcare in the past decade has not only created more jobs, money, and

3

services for the people, it has also created more inefficiencies and disorganization. The advent of new technology, the transformation of the reimbursement system, the demands to increase revenue and decrease cost, and the latest approaches to quality of care have contributed to new healthcare environments within which workers function and healthcare services are provided. The reimbursement changes of the 1980s and the mergers and acquisitions of the 1990s have significantly changed the healthcare industry's landscape. Reengineering has displaced employees and deprived them of jobs and job security, lowered their morale, and eroded their trust. Physician-hospital integrations have threatened physician autonomy and leadership and caused organizational conflicts. Integrated healthcare systems have become cumbersome to manage because, although integration unifies the best organizational and fiscal practices, it creates strategic conflicts and management problems, which are to be expected, but can nevertheless derail the smooth flow of the system and disrupt patient services. Amid these changes, healthcare leaders plowed through, weary and doubtful of their ability to rebuild trust and guide their organizations into the next century. These laments include:

"These are the toughest times I have ever faced in my 30 years in healthcare administration. Frankly, I am glad that I am nearing retirement."

"Twenty-five years ago our graduates were running hospitals within five years of graduation—and doing so quite effectively. Now I doubt that any but a handful will ever be able to fully comprehend the complexity of today's large healthcare enterprises."

"Our class read the Mintzberg article.[2] We all agreed that Mintzberg probably did not consider today's healthcare environment when he wrote this article.* We came to the conclusion that no one was well-suited to lead today's complex healthcare organizations."

"The stress, the lack of clarity, changing our vision every two to three years, our constant reengineering and restructuring—all this is taking its toll on our leadership. We are all physically and mentally exhausted and some of us are burned out. It's not fun anymore."

IMPERATIVE ACTIONS

The healthcare industry, its workers, and the people whom it serves need leaders who can rebuild trust, restore efficient processes, and ensure quality through rough organizational transitions and trends. This is the purpose of a leadership imperative. The following observations delineate the most prevalent obstacles that face leaders today. Each observation is coupled by an imperative.

Healthcare organizations today are more complex. Twenty-five years ago, healthcare organizations were not elaborate. Hospitals, doctor's offices, and nursing homes were the most ubiquitous embodiment of organizations. There were no healthcare *systems*, no integrated delivery networks, no IPAs, PHOs, MSOs, or POs. The hospital organization was not a conglomerate; it existed solely to provide care for the hospitalized patient; therefore, leaders weren't mired in the complications of

> Hospitals in America are significantly less efficient than they could and should be.
>
> George Halvorson[3]

---

*In the article, author Henry Mintzberg introduces covert leadership. Covert leadership is inconspicuous, but hands-on, management to allow employees to learn the intricacies of the job on their own and to be proud of it. However, this type of leadership would only work if the leader has an intimate understanding of all aspects of everything she/he is managing. Although this is an ideal type of leadership, it does not work in healthcare because too many changes occur in the industry. As a result, leaders cannot keep up and do not always have more information than her/his ward.

5

the organizational structure with its multiple business lines. The visions and missions of these simpler organizations were clear, as well.

The more complex the system, the less efficient its operation is an adage that's true of today's healthcare systems. Decreased efficiency then results in less satisfaction not only for the system's patients, but also its workers. Complex systems exhaust their leaders and their resources because they require more attention and focus. Therefore, some industry experts, and some observers, question the efficiency of integrating services. Some board members and senior leaders of large, well-known, highly-integrated systems privately express their concerns with what they have built. Management guru Peter Drucker points out: "The addition of each relay in an electronic circuit halves the amount of signal that passes through it, doubling the noise. And when a healthcare enterprise reaches a certain size and complexity, the message and value is also overwhelmed by the static."[4]

Imperative action: Restore the simplicity of the healthcare organization by clarifying the structure, mission and vision, and future direction.

Healthcare employee commitment and loyalty is at its lowest. Layoffs, downsizing, and reduced work hours, which are results of the changes and consequential severe reengineering, have taken their toll on healthcare workers: opinion surveys reveal employee morale is low, while unionization efforts are up, after a 20-year lull. In his book, *The Human Equation: Building Profits by Putting People First*, Jeffrey Pfeffer states that job security is one of the most important elements of a high-performance work environment.[5]

For a long time, the healthcare industry offered just that: job security; and employees showed their appreciation for it through loyalty to the organization. Employees stayed at their jobs longer, performed harder and better, recommended family members to open positions, missed fewer workdays, and participated more in the activities of the organization. Today, even the hardiest healthcare systems cannot ensure jobs for their employees. One CEO suggested that the high levels of trust between management and staff that once existed in the healthcare industry may never return: "I remember the first time I faced a room full of hospital employees who were to be laid off. That was in 1985 — and I personally talked to all of them. However, the last three times my organization has laid employees off, I did not even go to the sessions. I was told that it was legally risky and that it could be better handled by our human resources staff. We handed the laid-off employees to an outplacement firm to work with them. I feel like I abandoned them and feel really bad about this, but I don't know what to do about it."

Imperative action: Enlist the strong support of employees by enhancing trust levels and developing agendas in which they can participate, such as including them in certain decision-making roles.

Physicians today are generally dissatisfied with the management of the industry. At a recent medical staff quarterly meeting, a well-respected physician stood to proclaim "It is time that we take back control of healthcare — and it should start with our own health system!" Everyone in the room broke out in spontaneous applause. This sentiment, albeit revolutionary, reverberates the schism between healthcare leaders and physicians today. Much of this unrest stems from failed integration efforts.

Although physician integration aims to align common interests and goals, it may also reduce autonomy, complicate decision making, and contrast with the views of the physicians involved. As a result, physicians distrust the manner in which management operates the system and lose their faith and loyalty. If given a choice, physicians would rather elect another physician to lead the organization, as this actual sentiment from a hospital board

> A hospital is only a pile of bricks until people walk in in the morning. Yet it is amazing how this prime reality is forgotten, and how secondarily people are treated.
>
> V. Clayton Sherman[6]

member seconds: "I would agree. We seem to have forgotten our patients in our drive to build a bigger more comprehensive healthcare system. At least having a physician as our CEO would bring back that patient focus." Some experts believe that the integration efforts of the past several years have severely failed, as J. Daniel Beckham states, "Hospitals and physician practices are not good representations of tight coupling."[7]

Both the American College of Physician Executives (ACPE) and the American College of Healthcare Executives (ACHE) have experienced large increases in physician membership. Graduate schools throughout the country have developed management programs targeted at physicians. Many physicians enrolled in these management courses say that their motivation to attend is driven by their dissatisfaction with management of healthcare systems. In addition, many of them seek to improve healthcare organizations and the services they provide.

Imperative action: Improve relations with the physician collective. Consider that more and more physicians are qualified to move into more significant leadership roles.

Patients today are generally dissatisfied with the industry. Although much of the patient concerns relate to issues with their health insurance and HMOs, dissatisfaction with the poor quality of care and lack of attention in healthcare settings has recently come to the forefront. Many patients, who suffer from the decline, are cognizant of the reengineering efforts that result in downsizing, mergers, and worker and physician discontent. The recent report "1999 Environmental Assessment: Rising to the Challenge of a New Century" stated that the leading predictor of consumer satisfaction is when the healthcare worker shows concern for the patient's well-being.[8] Unfortunately, many patients today have been so overlooked that they cannot even conceive of well-being, let alone perceive it.

8

Many of our healthcare systems have grown so large that patients report a lack of responsiveness similar to that experienced with large corporations. One educated patient compared her experiences with one health system to "calling an 800 customer-service number in the middle of the night on Sunday."

Imperative actions: Address patient concerns, improve quality of care and consumer service, and establish a good relationship with the community you serve.

Healthcare executives today are generally dissatisfied with the industry. Numerous healthcare articles reveal that an increased number of executives have left the field because they are unhappy with the demands of their jobs. The most obvious reason, according to the book *Remaking Health Care in America,* may be that "the U.S. healthcare system is out of balance. The values underlying the system are not in harmony with each other." In addition, "these changes disrupt established norms, values, and behaviors of all parties, creating challenges that are similar to attempting to build a new house in the midst of an earthquake."[9] As evident in the laments of leaders above, leaders are stressed about doctoring their systems to meet the new demands and to appease everyone involved. Some are not confident about the future of their fields and some may have bought into the fear that the healthcare industry will continue to decline.

Imperative action: Invest time and resources to retain good executives by providing training and maintaining good relationships.

CONCLUSION

Aside from the perspectives discussed above, the ultimate reason for enhancing the skills of our healthcare leaders may be found in the comic strip character Dilbert because many Americans echo Dilbert's belief about management. In the spin-off book, *The Dilbert Principle*, creator Scott Adams writes: "The most ineffective workers are systematically moved to the place where they can do the least damage: management."[10] Although this sentiment certainly does not characterize most leaders, it reflects the public's jaded perception. Heeding the symptoms described above and prescribing both cures and preventative measures are the only ways to invalidate and combat these negative perceptions.

*   *   *

SELF-EVALUATION QUESTIONS

- Do I view myself as a leader? If so, is my goal to bring about needed change or, in the words of one CEO, "only to build palaces and monuments to my legacy?"
- Do I view leadership as an act, a process, or simply a skill?
- Do I, and do others, think that there is a leadership imperative today?
- Have I observed any significant shifts and trends within the industry and popular culture that affect leadership in my organization?
- Does it seem more difficult to lead and manage change today?

Chapter Two

THE VALUES-BASED DEFINITION

Disagreement about the definition of leadership stems from the fact that it involves a complex interaction among the leader, the followers, and the situation. Some researchers define leadership in terms of personality and physical traits, while others believe leadership is represented by a set of prescribed behaviors. In contrast, other researchers believe that the concept of leadership doesn't really exist. There is a common thread, however, among the definitions of leadership. The common thread is social influence.

Robert Kreitner and Angelo Kinicki[1]

THE CONCEPT OF LEADERSHIP is probably one of the most discussed and ultimately the most misunderstood topics. Is it an art, a science, or both? Do you define leadership based on a specific task? For example, are you a leader if you are in charge of guiding a team from Point A to Point B? Are you a leader only if you have followers? Can we measure your effectiveness based on your followers' accomplishments alone? For example, if your team reached Point B, are you a successful leader? And, does it matter how you got there?

As an executive search consultant, I've noticed that "you know what I mean" is one of the most repeated phrases during my discussions with employers. Although employers have their favorite general qualifications for leaders (e.g., must be "an outstanding leader," have "strong leadership skills," must have "integrity, high energy, and be a people person," "must be a team player and results-oriented"), they are often hard-pressed to provide more specific details on their meaning. As a result, they resort to replying "You know what I mean" when asked for more detail. After all these years, despite all the publications, seminars, speeches, and casual banter about the subject, no one is able to articulate a comprehensive, absolute definition of leadership.

Leadership is a living phenomenon; therefore, it is expected to shift its shape and mold itself into the demands of its followers or its purpose. This is probably why defining it is so difficult and why questions such as those we posed above remain unanswered. This chapter presents various definitions of leadership from many well-respected authors and will also attempt to define leadership by examining its closest ally—values. For the purposes of this book, the term values is used to refer to leadership values.

OTHER PERSPECTIVES

LEADERSHIP VERSUS MANAGEMENT THEORY

In his book, A Force for Change: How Leadership Differs from Management, John Kotter proposed that leadership is different from management because leadership is a process that focuses on making organizational changes, while management is primarily concerned with control and results. Although Kotter agrees that both responsibilities are important, he views leaders as the stimuli behind an organization's adoption of—and adaptation to—improved processes.[2] As a result, his readers are convinced that being a leader is preferable to being only a manager. The distinction, in my opinion, is clearly semantics because all leaders manage and all managers lead.

COMPREHENSIVE THEORY

Ralph Stogdill wrote what may be the most comprehensive treatise on leadership in his book *Stogdill's Handbook of Leadership: A Survey of Theory and Research*. In the book, Stogdill argues that leadership is any of the following:

- …a focus of team processes
- …personality and its effects
- …the art of inducing compliance
- …the exercise of influence
- …an act that results in others acting or responding in a shared direction
- …a form of persuasion
- …a power relation
- …an instrument of goal achievement
- …an emerging effect of interaction
- …a differentiated role
- …the initiation of structure
- …interaction between members of a team occurs when one team member modifies the motivation or competencies of others in the team…. Leaders are "agents of change, persons whose acts affect other people more than other people's acts affect them."[3]

This catalog not only defines the aspects of leadership, it also serves as a checklist. The conclusive quality of these definitions implies that if leaders would only improve in each one of these areas, they would be more effective. This is often called competency-based leadership. Although this view explains the technical aspects behind the concept of leadership, it ignores the art and the spiritual side, and doing so makes leadership seem mechanical.

PROCESS THEORY

In the book, *Organizational Behavior*, authors Robert Kreitner and Angelo Kinicki describe leadership as "a social influence process in which the leader seeks the voluntary participation of subordinates in an effort to reach organizational goals."[4]

This definition is true in three ways. First, leadership is a process because it takes place over a period of time, and it has a beginning and an end. The end is usually the point in time when a measure of leadership effectiveness may be ascertained. Second, leadership does not mean intimidation of followers into participation. Although some healthcare "leaders" may use force to coerce "volunteers," this technique is never acceptable because it is highly unethical. Third, this definition describes movement toward achievement, or progress-driven, which is another good measure of effectiveness.

CONTINGENCY THEORY

In this perspective, leadership is viewed on a contingency basis. That is, all leadership behaviors are always contingent upon these three primary variables:

(1) the leader
(2) the followers
(3) the situation

The contingency theory allows us to better understand why different types of leaders are needed for different types of situations and with different types of people. Some followers respond only to certain types of leaders. Different situations may require different leadership styles and different response from followers.

Contingency leadership, or situational leadership, simply suggests that "leader effectiveness is primarily determined by selecting the right kind of leader for a certain situation or changing the situation to fit the particular leader's style."[5] This school of thought purports that leaders must have versatility and be able to adapt to different types of followers, organizations, and situations. Although this approach has great merit and is the most validated theory of leadership, it fails to provide a focused picture of leadership.

MY THEORY

I contend that: (1) leadership is both inherent and learned, and (2) leadership values and skills are interrelated in that you cannot have one without the other. Numerous research studies suggest that many leadership skills and traits are the result of heredity.[6] In this vein, we can argue that those so-called born leaders who develop certain values early in life also tend to exhibit strong leadership characteristics and skills early. Others who did not develop these values early must cultivate them first to enhance their leadership capabilities, which is a belief that many managers, executives, and consultants—myself included—hold.

So, is there a definitive characteristic that differentiates strong leaders from weak leaders? Are there traits that drive the behavior of effective leaders? Do effective leaders possess something that average leaders do not? Yes is the only answer to these questions. Having the *correct leadership values* is the ultimate key.

Values, also known as guiding principles, are ingrained concepts and beliefs that guide our behavior and direct our thoughts. They are formed early in life and usually exist with little change for a lifetime. Because values serve as our moral framework, they help us analyze unexpected situations, make decisions during times of stress, and rise above difficult situations.

Values contain a judgmental element in that they carry an individual's ideas as to what is right, good, or desirable.

Stephen P. Robbins[7]

All people—leaders and followers alike—have values (and, I must point out, not necessarily positive ones). However, some are more predisposed than others to have values that affect their leadership effectiveness. For example, Leader A values being around other people, while Leader B values being alone. Because Leader A spends more time with others, she is exposed to others' ideas to which she may be more open, and she witnesses other practices—good and bad—from which she may learn. Leader B's values, on the other hand, may not be as effective for the development of leadership behavior because he is isolated from the opinions and experiences of others. The real "value" of values is the degree to which a leader will allow these values to influence her/him.

Our individual values influence how we perceive other people and teams. If leadership is a "social influence process," as Kreitner and Kinicki suggested, then values can affect it either negatively or positively. Leaders are the most influential when followers know what their leaders stand for because followers can either relate, or not relate, to the ideals of the leader. In addition, values guide the interactions between leaders and followers, serving as the "fluid" of the social interchange. Under the contingency theory, in which leaders consider all variables involved before making a decision and acting upon it, effective leaders ultimately rely on their personal values to steer them toward appropriate decisions.

IMPACT OF VALUES

The following are stages in the growth of leadership. The description of each stage shows how leaders progressively grow and develop (see Figure 2.1).

Unconscious Incompetence. "You don't know that you don't know." This is the most difficult stage for many leaders because they are unaware of their own mistakes and flaws. Often, they work in successful organizations and do not even consider that problems with their leadership skills might exist. Leaders who are most likely at this level are those who have not started to develop appropriate leadership values or may be highly resistant to the input and feedback of others. As a result, they need training and awareness to enhance their self-understanding.

Conscious Incompetence. "You know that you don't know." Although this stage is the most important step toward learning, it can be the most challenging because sometimes you have to lose your job first before you realize that your performance needs work. For others, this realization is a gradual process and may come as the result of the influence of a strong mentor or coach and a sincere desire to grow and improve.

Conscious Competence. "You know that you know." Although this stage comprises leaders who are neither born nor strong leaders, this is when they start developing and honing their potentials. Leaders at this stage work very hard to put into practice appropriate skills, but sometimes fail because the skills are not part of their natural thinking habits yet.

Unconscious Competence. "You don't know that you know." This is the ultimate stage of leadership development because the activities here flow smoothly with neither great force nor hesitation. Leaders at this level seem to be true naturals at their trade. This is truly descriptive of a "born leader."

CONCLUSION

Developing an operative definition of leadership is necessary for growth, so leaders must increase their knowledge and awareness by reading more books on the topic and explore more and various approaches to leadership. Leaders should personalize these definitions and theories to fit their own personal milieu

FIGURE 2.1
The Learning and
Mastery Process

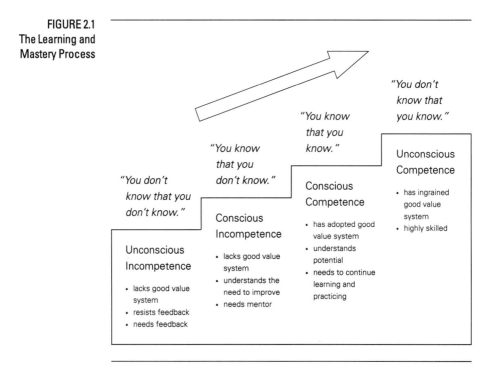

"You don't know that you know."

"You know that you know."

"You know that you don't know."

"You don't know that you don't know."

Unconscious Competence

- has ingrained good value system
- highly skilled

Conscious Competence

- has adopted good value system
- understands potential
- needs to continue learning and practicing

Conscious Incompetence

- lacks good value system
- understands the need to improve
- needs mentor

Unconscious Incompetence

- lacks good value system
- resists feedback
- needs feedback

and quest for self-improvement. Defining and evaluating your specific leadership skills is the first step toward improvement. Interact with other leaders and examine and discuss their strategies. Finally, observe your own impact within your organization.

By allowing positive values to influence you, you are also allowing better judgment into your style. Parts II and III of this book identify the values that must guide you as a leader and team member. Appendix C offers you an opportunity to assess your own professional and personal value system.

* * *

SELF-EVALUATION QUESTIONS

- What do I value? Do these values assist my leadership activities or hinder them?

- Do I have values or guiding principles that direct my behavior?
- Do I have personal values that may conflict with what I need to do as a leader?
- Have I ever written a narrative describing my leadership style? Did I do it primarily to impress a search consultant or a potential employer, or did I do it to evaluate my strengths and weaknesses?
- What is my definition of leadership?
- List several successful healthcare leaders. What do they all have in common?
- What are the values or guiding principles that successful leaders possess?
- In Chapter 1, you were asked if you viewed leadership as an act, a process, or simply a skill. Now that you have completed this chapter, answer the question again. How is your response different?

Chapter Three

THE SENIOR LEADER
PREDICAMENT

"Complacency is a deadly affliction for people and organizations, and healthcare organizations are not immune."

Jeff Goldsmith[1]

T HE TEMPERATURE OF THE HEAD is often a good
indicator of the temperature of the body. This truism
applies to healthcare organizations, as well. Therefore,
to better understand the handicap of a healthcare system, examining its highest commanders—the senior leaders—is imperative. Because the senior leadership team functions as the
primary decision makers and establishes the mission, vision, culture, and practices of an organization, should it also be accountable for the problems borne by their processes? Although
apportioning blame is not my intention, the question of accountability is this chapter's core. From late 1998 to early 1999,
I had a chance to interview, formally and informally, numerous

healthcare leaders to identify critical challenges in the next century.* This chapter gives voice to some of the major concerns gathered from those sessions.

One of the key concerns of many leaders is the declining, or poor, performance by their organization's senior-level leadership teams. Table 3.1 lists the current mindset—among caregivers, support teams, and leaders—within many healthcare organizations. I encourage you to create a similar table to help you identify the prevailing attitude in your own organization and determine the immediate and root causes of each.

LEADERSHIP PREDICAMENT

Although the healthcare environment is much different today and organizational problems exist in all industries, one of the reasons that chaos ensues is that senior leaders fail to anticipate, manage through, and rise above the inevitable changes in the industry. Unfortunately, many senior leaders have become so complacent with their skills and so overwhelmed by the daily rigors of their positions that instead of seeking creative solutions, they seek factors to blame—ranging from government regulations to declining reimbursement. However, in fairness to all senior leaders and teams, complex organizational factors do exist that impede their performance and render them ineffective. The following factors are what Fred Brown argues in the foreword that healthcare leaders must overcome.

COMPLEX ORGANIZATIONAL STRUCTURE

Alliances, affiliations, coalitions, and federations have greatly complicated healthcare management because they reinvented, as their nature decrees, how healthcare services are delivered,

---

*The materials were collected during several educational conferences and two CEO think-tank sessions. The comments present the collective thoughts of more than 50 senior-level leaders and do not portray the practices of any specific healthcare organization.

Mindset	Immediate Cause	Root Cause
Loss of trust	Layoffs	Frequent mid-course change of direction
Loss of loyalty and commitment	Constant downsizing	Frequent mid-course change of direction
Organizational chaos	Failed reengineering	Frequent mid-course change of direction
Lack of clear strategic direction	Frequent leadership turnover	Lack of leadership focus
Failed physician integration	Command and control atmosphere	Desire to control physicians
Stifled creativity	Fear and uncertainty about the future	No loyalty to organization
Distance between caregivers and leaders	Larger bureaucratic organizations	Drive to create larger healthcare organizations

TABLE 3.1
Organizational
Mindset and Causes

paid for, and measured. Consequently, the redesign of services created the need for managers to oversee the quality and flow of services. Ultimately, a complex network of managers who managed more managers emerged, which created a vast organizational maze.

In the early 1970s, the typical hospital organizational chart was intelligible (see Figures 3.1. and 3.2 for examples). Most hospitals had an administrator—which was the title most used for CEOs—who oversaw four to six other managers in charge of areas such as nursing, professional services, support services, and finance. Executives responsible for managed care, marketing, PHOs, and MSOs did not exist. At that time, only a few nursing

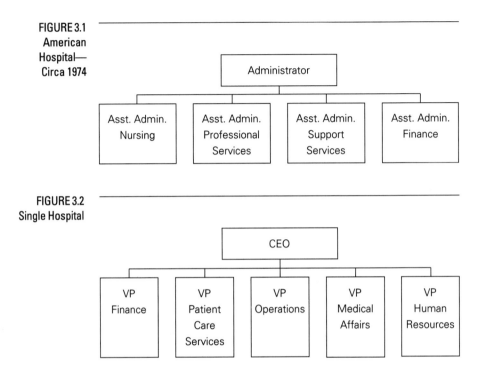

FIGURE 3.1
American
Hospital—
Circa 1974

FIGURE 3.2
Single Hospital

administrators held expanded responsibilities in other patient care service areas.

Today, many hospitals have become health systems and are often saddled with multiple business lines. Contradictory payment schemes, such as fee-for-service and capitation, exist and internal operations have been reengineered. This expansion has created a schism between leaders who oversee only external transactions—physician practice acquisitions, alliances, mergers and acquisitions, new business lines, etc. — and leaders who are involved exclusively in mundane internal operations. As is the case with anything new, management of external services is considered prestigious and glamorous. As a result, senior leaders who manage internal affairs resent the managers of those new services. One COO confessed: "We run internal operations and are expected to finance the outside businesses that seem to operate at great losses. We are very tired of this scenario!"

The rapid growth of the healthcare system has also diversified and enlarged the size of the typical senior leadership team. As a result, the personal and professional camaraderie that used to bind senior leaders is almost extinct, and the meetings have become too large for intimate and goal-driven interaction. Some teams convene as many as 22 people at the conference table.

UNFAMILIAR ENVIRONMENT

Complicated payment systems, increased emphasis on quality and satisfaction measurements, and introduction of care maps and clinical pathways are only some of the unfamiliar situations that senior leaders encounter today. Because the senior leaders often have no knowledge of or experience with the matters on hand, decisions are often based on a best-guess-decision matrix, which is not only risky but potentially fatal to the organization.

Legal issues further complicate decision-making processes. Numerous senior leaders reveal that most decisions today are weighed by their legal ramifications. One CEO is concerned that the "mission too often takes the back seat to legal maneuvering."

FAST PACE OF CHANGE

The traditional mindset of many healthcare organizations is to follow predictable, tried processes; therefore, many of its leaders are reluctant to adopt innovative or even alternative methods of operation. Fax machines, mobile telephones, and e-mails further encourage this pursuit and embody the speed of decision making in today's environment—the fax-like speed. However, senior leaders must keep pace with the industry's rapid revolution because leaders who are unable to create or activate future vision are the biggest liabilities. Therefore, they must make quick decisions to ensure that their organizations stay informed, move in the right direction, and possibly stride ahead of the competition.

What suffers in this equation is the quality of the decisions. Senior leaders cannot consult adequately on each issue because time does not allow for lengthy reflection. A CEO from the Midwest admitted that her board is often frustrated with the number of decisions that her team makes on significant issues without thoughtful deliberation. Decision making without proper analysis is prevalent in any industry despite the proliferation of information available today via the Internet and other multimedia sources. Even graduate schools offer more courses that focus on how to make decisions with limited information.

LACK OF TIME

Many CEOs agree that lack of time is their biggest adversary. If the ability to stop time could be bottled and sold, it would sell out even before the cap is twisted closed. Some of its first buyers would certainly be CEOs and their team members. Their concern, however, is no longer focused on managing time efficiently, but instead on understanding how to resolve so many issues within limited time. As the industry transforms, more decisions need to be made at an increasingly faster rate. As a result, more senior leaders get burned-out by the constant pressure.

Lack of time leads to:

(1) **Communication problems.** Because the meeting agenda lists so many pressing issues, not all members of the leadership team can convey their thoughts. Even those who have the opportunity to do so cannot properly elaborate on their ideas. On the other hand, some leaders may counter that too much time is spent on meeting minutia that less time is appropriated for actual strategy evaluation.

2. **Less interaction among senior leaders.** Front-line leadership teams spend more time working together than do senior leadership teams. Many senior teams come together only on a "part-time" basis and, as a result, they are less familiar and friendly with each other. Personal and professional conflicts tend to exist more, and can be more volatile, within these estranged teams. In this type of environment, insider knowledge becomes a capricious power with which to intimidate and subdue the opposing members. Withholding of knowledge becomes more frequent.

LACK OF SHARED VISION

Goals are achievable only when everyone on a team is deeply committed to them. Unfortunately today, many senior leaders move in opposite directions, harbor personal agendas, and have little personal or professional compatibility with colleagues. While some leaders focus on external business development activities, others commit to managing acute care outcomes. Goals such as improving health system performance or enhancing patient satisfaction are more abstract than the goals set out by lower-level teams within the organization. The threat, and possibility, of losing an organizational position, which is brought on by unpredictable mergers and structural reorganizations, has turned some leaders into fierce competitors and has created a negative political landscape.

INAPPROPRIATE COMPENSATION

Compensation can cause severe division, infighting, jealousy, and mistrust among senior leaders. Compensation is often highly subjective; in some organizations, much of it is often determined at the whim of its CEOs. Senior leaders have overlapping corporate and individual goals and their performance goals are less tangible; hence, their performance is harder to measure. Unfortunately, leaders' compensation is based more on market standards than on their performance as team members. Most compensation is contained within the base salary and the small part that is sometimes determined by incentives is not significant enough to carry great weight with executives. The incentive plans place greater emphasis on individual objectives, behavior, and performance than on the individual's performance and behavior within a team. The few team-incentive plans that do exist are often so broad that they do not focus on the individual's behavior within the team, but on organization-wide performance over which many of the team members have no influence.

IMBALANCE OF POWER

Different levels of titles, such as senior VP or executive VP, within a leadership team connote varying degrees of authority. This creates imbalance and defeats the purpose of an equal, cooperative setting. Some leadership teams are seriously out of balance in that some leaders are tenured because they have been serving longer, while some leaders are more respected or naturally "stronger" because of their position in the organization or team such as being the CFO or COO. While this mix seems necessary and useful to a leadership team, it often alienates other members who have neither tenure nor higher-level position.

MEDIOCRE CEOS

In an ideal world, mediocre CEOs do not exist. However, in the real world mediocre CEOs abound. How does this happen? Complacency about the way things work is the main answer. Consider the following complacent scenarios:

- Some organizations retain mediocre CEOs because they have never seen a pressing need to make a change. These organizations often are successful despite their poor CEOs.
- Some CEOs' mediocrity is never revealed because they know how to isolate themselves from review and criticism by using other people or circumstances to shield their inability. As board leadership changes, some of these CEOs are able to hang on to their positions for years.
- Many organizations hire the wrong types of CEO for their respective organization's need and culture. A proper place for everyone—this should be one of the basic rules when hiring for a leadership position. Unfortunately, when an improper hiring occurs, organizations tend to stick with their mistake and hope that the situation improves.
- Problems also occur when CEOs grant episodic, rather than functional, authorization. When decisions are made on an individual basis, inconsistency ensues, which creates a problem for the senior leadership team because no general standards exist that they can follow. The senior executives are then forced to spend unnecessary time mired in organizational politics and "protecting their back."

CONCLUSION

My intent in this chapter is not to accuse senior leaders of contributing to the issues that plague healthcare today. My intent is twofold: (1) to expose the root causes of why people—workers, patients, and leaders alike—are dissatisfied and why so much finger pointing occurs within the healthcare industry; and (2) to provide a forum in which we can discuss ways to correct, or lessen, these organizational and professional deficiencies. One of the most important characteristics of strong leaders is their ability to objectively analyze and assess their performance and their impact on their organization. Evaluate yourself with the various assessment tools provided in Part IV of this book. Consider the concepts in this chapter and apply them to your organization. I will have done my job if you agree to at least one of the arguments presented here.

* * *

SELF-EVALUATION QUESTIONS

- How influential is the senior leadership team in my organization?
- Does the frequent turnover among senior leadership team members create a serious, negative effect on the team's effectiveness? Why?

PART II

Personal Values

Chapter Four

RESPECT AND STEWARDSHIP

Being in a position to exercise power over other people may be satisfying for a little while, but never in the long run. Ultimately it leaves you lonely. You command, and you receive fear and obedience in return, and what emotionally healthy person can live on a diet of fear and obedience?

Harold S. Kushner[1]

I F LEADERSHIP IS A JOURNEY, then respect for its constituents is its fuel and good stewardship is its compass. Without respect for others and good stewardship, leadership is a farcical, stagnant voyage. Respect is the value that multiplies each person's desire to deliver better, harder, and consistently excellent performance.

STEWARDING WITH RESPECT

Stewardship, or leadership, is traditionally perceived as a prestigious position filled by influential people whose main role in goal accomplishment is to give orders. This controlling and

33

manipulative concept may not be as prevalent now because more leaders are becoming aware that this type of management begets only few and very uneasy followers. When stewardship is selfish, it is frequently rejected by society. According to recent polls, many Americans distrust and are cynical about leaders in all types of industries and organizations. These negative attitudes have been exacerbated by various events in the 1990s including peccadilloes of politicians and endless expansions by seemingly greedy CEOs and corporations.

Respect for self and others is the nucleus in all activities. It is a value that commands leaders to restrain ego, to admit mistakes, to pay attention, to care for and honor others, to keep an open mind, to give credit or compliment, and to ask for help or insight. Stewards must return to this basic value to regain trust and to amplify their effectiveness. Although the task is daunting, it is one of the most worthwhile undertakings.

SELF-ESTEEM VERSUS SELF-CENTEREDNESS

Stewardship begins with the willingness to be accountable for some larger body than ourselves—an organization, a community. Stewardship springs from a set of beliefs about reforming organizations that affirms our choice for service over the pursuit of self-interest.

Peter Block[2]

Self-esteem is an individual's respect for her/his own convictions, actions, imperfections, and abilities. Without self-esteem, an individual is not mentally healthy; does not function well under pressure; cannot accept or give compliments and criticism; and tends to be more egotistical, controlling, and in constant need of affirmation. Self-centeredness, on the other hand, is an individual's overly favorable concept of her/his own abilities, views, decisions, and needs. Self-centered people are arrogant, insecure while feeling superior, and, in effect, harmful to any social setting. Leaders without self-esteem harm the organization because:

- they do not respect others;
- they alienate others with their domineering attitude;
- they exasperate others by demanding so much approval for their every action;

- they cause unnecessary work and spend time unnecessarily to repair mistakes caused by their inability to have faith in others' work; and
- they engender disloyalty and fear.

OPERATIONALIZE THE CONCEPT

Consider the following ways that you, the steward, can employ respect in various facets of your position.

Become a collaborator. Collaboration is a partnership among people who have distinct or shared knowledge about the goal they are trying to accomplish. The reasons for collaboration are to combine expertise; share experience; minimize mistakes; prevent wasted effort, time, and money; and produce a better result. Leaders who become good collaborators learn to:

> Collaborative people are those who identify a possibility and recognize that their own view, perspective, or talent is not enough to make it a reality.
>
> Robert Hargrove[3]

(1) not provide their own opinion prior to hearing others';
(2) be active listeners who constantly try to better understand what others say;
(3) reflect on what others say before responding; and
(4) ask questions during discussions because of actual inquisitiveness, not doubt.

Although leaders sometimes collaborate with those in lower-level positions, they must push the hierarchy within the organization to permeate the structure of the partnership. Why is this necessary? Because collaboration is about equal exchange of ideas. Leaders must respect the opinions and suggestions of everyone with whom they collaborate, regardless of positions in the organizational structure.

Show respect by practicing respect. Respect often means different things to different people. For example, one person may define respect as being asked his opinion, while another person

35

may view respect as being empowered. So, find out what others mean by respect and learn how to show it appropriately.

Respect often depends on certain conditions or positions. For example, a judge in his courtroom demands a stricter sense of respect. However, outside of work the same judge demands a more relaxed respect, although not any less. Unfortunately, respect to those in lower-level service positions seems nonexistent in many industries. Professors and students alike may not show respect for their university's security personnel or maintenance staff. In the healthcare industry, physicians are traditionally more respected than nurses because of their position and status.

One of the most universal ways to show respect in the workplace is recognizing good work. Leaders typically employ others who handle situations while they themselves develop and articulate or implement the mission and vision of the organization. When asked about how he shows respect, a successful CEO offered: "I hire the very best people I can find, and then I show them the respect they are due by staying out of their way and letting them do their jobs." Another successful CEO revealed: "All of my executive team members think and act like each is my COO—and most importantly, they make most of their decisions without my involvement." These two quotes exemplify how leaders can show respect by empowering their staff.

In the book *Protocols for Healthcare Executive Behavior*, I suggested that adherence to many of the unwritten rules of society and organizations contribute to leadership success: "Unfortunately, there are no established codes of conduct that govern all of the various behavioral expectations of business situations. No rules or standards can cover every possible situation [that] executives encounter. However, our society does have certain principles that determine socially acceptable behavior."[4] A significant part of protocols involves courtesy that naturally evolves out of respect of other people.

1. Give compliments, be courteous, and show good manners and pleasant deportment to show that you appreciate and honor the efforts that others bring to the organization.
2. Learn the strength of collective action through the cooperative work of teams.
3. Take time out and go out of your way to ask for and listen to what others value, need, and expect.
4. Participate in others' activities to show you care about their interests.

Build extensive feedback systems. This is not intended to suggest a new and better performance evaluation program. Instead, the best feedback systems are those that provide constant, unfiltered, direct feedback and, when necessary, criticism. Feedback should be given on an ongoing basis and should be informal. The person evaluated should be given an opportunity to respond, ask questions, or simply state that the feedback was understood so that both parties involved agree.

In the book *Beyond Ambition: How Driven Managers Can Lead Better and Live Better,* author Robert E. Kaplan proposes that although giving feedback is difficult for every manager in an organization, senior leaders find receiving and giving it even harder because they are more isolated.[5] The few interactions that these leaders have with others usually take place in the executive suite, which is a setting that can render anyone intimidated and alienated. These leaders also have the power to hire and fire people. As a result of these trappings of power, leaders often cannot evaluate their staff properly and vice versa.

Although this difficulty may be the case for some senior leaders, receiving frequent input—and criticisms—from all levels of workers within the organization remains necessary because it is a sign of respect for others' opinions. Leaders would be more accepted, better informed, and easily evaluated if they were to interact more frequently outside of their offices and become more involved in all aspects of the organization. Isolation has trapped many otherwise effective leaders.

Learn to be genuine. Some have called this "authentic presence." Leaders can show genuineness by being involved and interested in their work and in the work of those around them without being intrusive and pretentious. The unspoken sentiment that springs from this involvement is: We are in this together. Many CEOs can attribute their acceptance and successes to having "walked the talk"* with people at all levels in the organization. In Catholic hospitals, nuns are known to be extraordinary influences because they are frequently visible and consistently approachable. Physicians tend to gravitate toward physician leaders who still maintain some clinical practice because these leaders can relate to their experiences, represent their needs, understand their issues, and defend their demands. Finding this commonality among people within the organization by being true to oneself and others is what every leader must master. As adults, we forget the basic principles of living that we learned as children: give back what you borrowed and respect your elders. As adults, we overlook simple explanations — such as the following dialogue from *The Velveteen Rabbit* by Margery Williams — to becoming better people.[6]

"What is REAL?" Asked the Rabbit one day. "Does it mean having things that buzz inside you and a stick-out handle?"

"Real isn't how you are made," said the Skin Horse. "It's a thing that happens to you.

---

*Management by Walking Around (MBWA) has become a popular trend among executives over the past decade. Its primary purpose is for executives to witness the effectiveness or ineffectiveness of various programs that their organization initiated or sponsor by visiting locations in which these services are performed. Although MBWA allows the executive to gain insight about and get familiar with settings that she/he will not normally visit, MBWA should not be done solely to increase visibility.

"Does it hurt?" asked the Rabbit.

"Sometimes," said the 'Skin Horse, for he was always truthful. "When you are Real you don't mind being hurt."

"Does it happen all at once, like being wound up," he asked, "or bit by bit?"

"It doesn't happen all at once," said the Skin Horse. "You become. It takes a long time.

That's why it doesn't often happen to people who break easily, or have sharp edges, or who have to be carefully kept… once you are Real you can't be ugly, except to people who don't understand."

Learn to value the output of others. The mark of a great leader becomes clear when she/he recognizes the excellent performance of someone else and allows others to shine for their accomplishment. This simple acknowledgment is one of the most powerful motivators that is much quieter than a standing ovation but more valuable than money.

Help others. This should become the leader's motto. Many leaders have studied coaching to enhance their abilities to evaluate, constructively criticize, and assist their staff. By helping others, the leader is saying: I admire and respect your work, and I'd like to help you attain and learn more.

Enhance your self-awareness. Leaders must be able to look inward to discover their strengths, weaknesses, goals, and impetus. Creativity often springs from being self-aware.

Take responsibility for mistakes and learn to apologize. This is often the most overlooked way of showing respect. Many

Leaders are best when people barely know they exist, not so good when people obey and acclaim them, worse when people despise them. But of good leaders, who talk little, when their work is finished, their aim fulfilled, the others will say 'We did this ourselves.'

Lao Tzu

39

leaders fail to realize that by simply owning up to their mistakes and apologizing, they are loudly proclaiming that they are penetrable, they are vincible, and they are human; hence, on the same level as others. What others hear when leaders say "I made a mistake and I'm sorry" is "I respect you, so I will not pretend or make you believe that what happened was your responsibility."

Learn the principle of affirmation. The word "affirm" comes from an ancient legal principle that decrees that the higher court must approve the decision of the lower court. In this parallel, leaders function as the higher court that must approve the work and contributions of their constituents. These affirmations always serve as a powerful, positive message and a great motivator for better performance.

Show appreciation. A note of congratulations, appreciation, or gratitude has always been a staple of good camaraderie. Although many leaders still make time to hand-write notes, this practice has declined and has taken the form of either a phone call or an e-mail message. Nevertheless, the idea is the same: a small token—a short note, a pat on the back, kind words, or a handshake—make a big impression on the recipient.

Show enthusiasm. Some leaders deem the showing of enthusiasm as inappropriate, unprofessional, and silly. However, many good leaders find setting goals and achieving them not only exciting but also satisfying. As a result, they become enthusiastic and spirited about their endeavors. In addition, leaders who show enthusiasm for their work tend to have a more positive environment and good-natured, loyal followers.

Showing enthusiasm and support for the mission of the organization is also important. Although this may be more applicable to leaders below the level of the CEO, CEOs must also be mindful of how they show support because the rank and file can view their leaders with skepticism if strong support is not shown for the mission.

Attendance at employee events is one area in which many senior executives fail. Failure to make an appearance—and an enthusiastic one—at employee, volunteer, or community events may negate many of the achievements of the leader. In addition, this lack of concern for activities that do not revolve around the power structure is disrespectful, as one executive's flippant remark expressed: "I really see no sense in serving hot dogs at the employee picnic. Let others handle that and I'll handle my responsibilities."

CONCLUSION

The concept of respect in stewardship is common-sense knowledge to some. However, this value is the hardest to master because it is imbedded in all the activities of a leader. In addition, it is also the hardest to sell because many have become too cynical and too uncomfortable to explore and analyze their inner workings, too complacent to change their strategies, too arrogant to evaluate their performance, and too impatient to learn new tricks. But respect in stewardship is not just a trick, it is a fundamental factor in any responsibility.

* * *

SELF-EVALUATION QUESTIONS

- What does respect mean to me?
- Can I respect others and still be accountable for their actions?
- Stewardship often sounds as if it has religious connotations. How do I define it?
- Do I have an appropriate feedback mechanism to assess how others view me?

Chapter Five

ETHICS AND INTEGRITY

Integrity implies clarity of values and/or direction, and behaviors consistent with them. While flexibility in thinking
and approaches to challenges is an enormous asset for
today's leaders, those who would follow their lead must be
able to perceive in these leaders a core consistency in their
fundamental values and actions.

Martin D. Merry[1]

A S ARE OTHER LEADERSHIP VALUES, ethics and integrity are interrelated. Ethics is a person's moral scope
and integrity is the person's capacity for staying within
that moral scope. Although the general concept of both values
is comprehensible, their true meaning is elusive. This chapter
explores the tandem nature of ethics and integrity, and provides

a guide for leaders on how to practice ethical behavior within the constructs of daily operation.

DEFINITIONS

Practically all leaders would consider themselves to possess high integrity. However, when asked about the integrity of other leaders, many state that leaders with high integrity are hard to find. Why the contradiction? Two reasons are plausible.

First, many definitions for integrity exist, but not one of them is universal. The *Merriam-Webster's Collegiate Dictionary, Tenth Edition* defines it as "the quality or state of being complete or undivided."[4] Some people define it as the ability to be absolutely honest; some measure it on an all-or-none scale; and others view it as a degree of genuineness. Because all people have their own definition, integrity in others is harder to gauge or "find" than integrity within ourselves. For example, I think that integrity is how I can differentiate right from wrong, and what drives me to strive for the right choices and behavior. Given my definition then, I can only find this definition within, and expect it from, myself.

A second reason other leaders do not see integrity in others is that each person perceives her/his own ethical standards depending on the situation at hand and the resulting consequences. Although everyone has her/his own concept of right and wrong, humans stray occasionally from their own standards. For example, if Leader A, who is regularly lauded for her good ethical judgment, occasionally makes personal copies on the organization's copy machine or makes personal calls on the corporate calling card, will she be considered unethical? Although Leader A's moral compass dictates that her actions are inappropriate, she continues to do it because she does not deem it harmful to the organization. This is an example of ethical relativism or contingency leadership. It provokes leaders into considering their own ethical anchors before facing complex situations.

Hypocrisy, by its very nature, is self-invalidating. It is mind rejecting itself. A default on integrity undermines me and contaminates my sense of self. It damages me as no external rebuke or rejection can damage me.

Nathaniel Branden[2]

Leaders who do not behave ethically do not demonstrate true leadership.

J. M. Burns[3]

44

OPERATIONALIZE THE CONCEPT

Unlike any other activities by leaders, the ethical decisions of leaders, especially senior leaders, are observed more closely — and are likely to be more critiqued — by everyone in the organization. These ethical dilemmas bear significant personal and professional risk because the resolutions to them often necessitate leaders to reveal their private opinions. So how can leaders lessen this risk but still handle these ethical challenges? The following guides show how.

Adopt an organizational code of ethics. A code of ethics defines appropriate, inappropriate, and gray areas of conduct within the organization. It is a set of laws that protects the organization from legal entanglement and protects employees from harassment and unfair treatment. Leaders should be enlisted to support it and should educate themselves and others about its application and benefit. Mechanisms that would monitor employee adherence to the code must be developed, as well. The Code of Ethics and Ethical Policy Statement of the American College of Healthcare Executives (ACHE) — the leading organization of healthcare executives — is an excellent guide for healthcare professionals who are seeking to expand their knowledge about ethical behaviors. As a result of government investigations in the 1990s, many healthcare organizations have developed corporate compliance, or responsibility, programs such as the very excellent one shown in Figure 5.1 from Catholic Healthcare Partners of Cincinnati, Ohio. Ultimately, the codes of ethics and compliance programs should be instituted because doing so is the right thing and is beneficial to the organization and its constituents as a whole, and not merely to impress investigators.

Adopt a personal code of ethics. Write on paper your own code of ethics and integrity. Address questions such as What do you

[Integrity is] accepting full responsibility, communicating clearly and openly, keeping promises, avoiding hidden agendas, and having the courage to lead yourself and your team or enterprise with honor, which includes knowing and being consistently honest with yourself, not only in mind but heart.

Robert K. Cooper and Ayman Sawaf[5]

FIGURE 5.1
Example of Code
of Conduct

1. Maintain a culture that values honesty, integrity, and ethics. Demonstrate those traits at every level of leadership.
2. Preserve and protect the organization's assets. Use resources carefully, according to ethical and legal standards.
3. Obey all laws and regulations.
4. Keep information about patients, associates and the organization confidential.
5. Avoid what are—or seem to be—conflicts of interest in your actions and dealings with others.
6. Maintain an environment where everyone is treated with dignity and respect and where the hallmark is high-quality, holistic care.

Source: Reprinted with permission from Catholic Healthcare Partners. 1998. *Corporate Responsibility: Core Values in Action.*

stand for? In what situations are you willing to be compromised? Where are you willing to cut corners?

Starting your own code of ethics not only resounds what is really important to you, but guides you in prioritizing and articulating when difficult issues come up. In adopting your own code, consider how others perceive your behavior and action because their opinion is important. As one CEO simply put it, "What would others think of you if they saw you or found out?"

Weigh the cost of not being ethical. If you were caught in a dubious scheme, such as misappropriating funds, or behaving badly, such as mistreating others, how would others react? Ask yourself the consequences first: "What is the downside risk in my behavior or actions?"; "What happens if I get caught?"; and "Is the payoff worth my career, my reputation, my livelihood?"

Tell the truth; don't exaggerate. In the strict ethical sense, telling the truth and not exaggerating are the same. Many people, however, differentiate the two. The argument for the difference is that telling the truth means telling no lies. On the other hand, exaggerating means stretching the truth to achieve a certain outcome or reaction. For many, including healthcare executives, the latter has become accepted, commonplace practice. Many executives overestimate, engage in hyperbole, bend the facts, provide misquotes, twist the truth, and inappropriately expand their commentary to fit their needs. Whether discussing budget or organizational performance, many communications are filled with subjective stretches of the reality. Consider the following simple, but powerful, comments that are often rhetorical overstatements:

- "We have cut all the fat out of our budgets. All that remains is absolutely necessary."
- "I have told the team that many, many times. They must not be hearing me."
- "I don't think I can cut any deeper—it will hurt patient care."
- "*Everyone* is very upset about this."

How many times have you heard these or similar comments and how many times have you fully believed them?

Do as you say. Become known as a leader with follow-through. Often, integrity is measured less by failures in large significant areas and more by the lack of follow-up on little items. If a promise is made, it should be honored.

Use power appropriately. Effective leaders are acutely aware that power can be used for good or bad. They understand the sources and uses of their power, and they use it very judiciously. Unfortunately, ineffective leaders and many of those new to leadership positions love to show their power to try to gain respect, prestige, and favors.

Admit mistakes. Perhaps one of the most powerful actions leaders can take is to admit mistakes. However, too many believe

47

that doing so decreases their power. The opposite is true; power is not incrementally earned by perfection. Instead, power is what followers bestow upon leaders. Followers of leaders who admit mistakes agree that admission of fault actually serves to increase their leader's power.

March to the beat of a different drummer. If your values of integrity and ethics are clear, then you know why you do what you do. Consequently, your behavior comes more naturally and you follow the "beat of your own drum." You are less likely to copy the person down the hall or at the other healthcare system. As a result, your actions take on their own integrity. When you establish your own ethics and integrity, you do not have to be concerned with what others think nor will you follow their lead.

Neither shall you allege the example of the many as an excuse for doing wrong.

Exodus 23:2

Be trustworthy. Author Stephen Covey describes being trustworthy as the embodiment of ethics and integrity. A leader is only as effective as the support that her/his followers grant her/him. Gaining that support is not possible if the leader does not earn others' trust and loyalty.

Manage expense accounts judiciously. Leaders must require approvals for all reimbursement, especially for petty cash funds. This simple system of fund management does not create more bureaucracy, but prevents temptation, and ensures that no one can question whether fund violation occurred. Seasoned leaders agree that mismanagement of expenses is one of the most common occurrences in organizations because it is so easy to overlook and undermine.

Minimize — or eliminate — excessive perqs and benefits. Our healthcare industry is earmarked by a high degree of accountability to our communities. Most healthcare organizations have been established as 501(c)(3) corporations; as such, no part of the net income is allowed to "inure" or be paid to individuals. However, recent surveys indicate that significant perquisites and benefits are provided to some executives who are already highly paid. While reasonable justification may exist for many of these bonuses, the appropriateness of some is highly questionable. Eliminating, or at least reducing, these perqs will demonstrate that high standard of service does not have to cost the organization a high price.

CONCLUSION

One of the greatest compliments to a leader is when others recognize her/his ethical uprightness. No matter what definition applies, the bottom line is ethics and integrity are always excellent ingredients in any leadership undertaking. Leaders become great leaders when they follow their own moral instincts. This makes them more focused during reorganization. This makes them more resourceful through times of deficiencies. This makes them more open-minded to change.

*　*　*

SELF-EVALUATION QUESTIONS

- What would others say about my integrity? About my ethics?
- Does integrity really mean that much to me? How many times have I not followed through? not done what I said I would do? not gotten back to someone when I promised I would?
- It is said that "actions speak louder than words." Viewed in this light, how do I stack up?
- Do I use the power granted to me appropriately?
- Have I ever "cut corners" and behaved in an ethically questionable manner?

Chapter Six

INTERPERSONAL CONNECTION

Of course, we do not live alone on islands.... We are born into families; we grow up into societies.... Once into our professions, we find that our jobs require us to interact frequently and effectively with others. If we fail to learn and apply the principles of interpersonal effectiveness, we can expect our progress to slow or stop.

Stephen R. Covey[1]

T HE HEALTHCARE SYSTEM is the true industry of the people. No other industry witnesses human afflictions — from diseases of the body to diseases of the spirit; hosts the most basic human need — interaction at the most inopportune moments; and serves as the most common human thread — everyone needs healthcare. Because of these truths, people — patients, employees, physicians, contractors, communities — are the critical factor in organizational success.

The irony is although many leading healthcare organizations find that improving relationships with their employees and patients is the key to excellence, most still focus on financial factors to measure their success. Every organization has an annual financial audit, but only a few conduct annual human resources audits, much less even define what these human resources audits might be. Almost every board of trustees has a finance committee, but only a few have human resources committees. This chapter reiterates the significance of having people skills—a value so subtle that it can be so easily undermined, but so powerful that it can make or break an organization.

PEOPLE SKILLS

Leaders who have "people skills" are marked by a profound respect for others' character and faith in their potential, which is why they enjoy being with people and interact well with them. Often, the primary deciding factor in an executive search is the candidate's "chemistry" or ability to "blend" with others. Although almost all organizations place good people skills at the top of their requirement list, they do not emphasize its importance to their existing employees and do not provide appropriate tools to measure people who possess it. Figure 6.1 exemplifies what healthcare leaders mean by good people skills.

OPERATIONALIZE THE CONCEPT

The backbone of people skills is reciprocity because without it no interaction or relationship occurs. Every healthy relationship—personal or professional—is marked by a mutual exchange—a quid pro quo of sorts. This exchange strengthens the bond and encourages its duration. Non-responsive, non-involved rank and file can discourage even the most interactive leader.

The following suggest ways you can enhance your interpersonal connections.

Leadership is a reciprocal relationship between those who choose to lead and those who decide to follow. Any discussion of leadership must attend to the dynamics of this relationship.

James Kouzes and Barry Posner[2]

FIGURE 6.1
Healthcare Leaders'
Definition of Good
"People Skills"

"They listen to others because they care what others have to say."

"They practice reflective listening and internalize what others are telling them."

"They don't always have to be right; they are willing to confront their humanness. They will readily admit their mistakes."

"They are appropriately assertive. You know where they stand on an issue." "You do not have to guess what they want or how they feel."

"They exhibit warmth, caring, and concern for others. They are not selfish."

"There is an air of genuineness about them. You can count on what they say."

"I can teach young executives almost anything—technical skills, healthcare knowledge, board and medical staff principles—but I cannot teach anyone how to get along with others. If they do not bring that to the job already, I cannot guarantee their success."

"They are open and approachable and really care about developing and sustaining strong interpersonal relationships."

Listen. Many leaders are leaders because they are the people in the know or they have answers to most organizational questions. Consequently, they do too much of the talking, especially with subordinates, and not enough of the listening. Hearing is easy because it is merely mechanical. Listening, on the other hand, is a process that not only demands your patience, time, energy, and respect to understand what others are telling you, it also demands your reaction and action to what you have been told. Listening, unlike hearing, is much more than a physical response. Leaders must especially listen to concerns that cannot be heard and behavior that cannot be seen. Although listening

HOW TO
ENHANCE YOUR
LISTENING
SKILLS

- Ask lots of questions. Try to avoid revealing an opinion on an issue through the tone or content of the question.
- Ask clarifying questions. Do not assume that all problems are the same.
- Ask reflective questions. Do so by trying to restate what is believed to be said by the other individual.
- Be open-minded.
- Be receptive to bad news. (This is particularly important for senior leaders.)
- Minimize your interruptions.
- Look for—ask for—suggestions.
- Involve others in conversations.

No matter how ambitious, capable, clear-thinking, competent…and witty you are, if you don't relate well to other people, you won't make it. No matter how professionally competent, financially adept, and physically solid you are, without an understanding of human nature, a genuine interest in the people around you, and the ability to establish personal bonds with them, you are severely limited in what you can achieve.

D. A. Benton[3]

is one of the most difficult tasks to master, especially in a high-stress, fast-paced environment, it is the most worthwhile skill. The techniques for enhanced listening are simple, but they are not always practiced.

Show respect. The title of the book *Lions Don't Need to Roar* is suggestive of the appropriate approach to other people. Author D. A. Benton suggests that "sincerity and positive regard are two things that just can't be faked, and you need both to deal with people effectively." Strong leaders almost always have great regard for others. They listen to their ideas, hear their concerns, and show care for their well-being. When asked what bothers them most about senior leadership, many employees often state that their senior leaders do not have respect for what they do "in the trenches." Often this means that the employees simply do not believe that their leaders understand the challenges or stress involved in their jobs. Hence, the employees do not feel respected.

Take time for people. The life of many senior executives is amazingly hectic, which leaves them no time to interact with others. This creates a perception among staff that their leaders

54

do not value them; they are merely cogs in the organizational machine; and questions (seen as interruptions), no matter how important, are not welcome. Executive parking spaces close to the entrance of the building or executive/physician dining rooms further remove senior leaders from the rank and file and add to this sense of alienation. Employee opinions of senior leaders in smaller organizations are almost always more positive than in larger ones because a smaller staff size affords leaders the opportunity to mingle, communicate, and listen more frequently. Leaders with strong people skills demonstrate a relaxed persona and create a more positive environment in which employees feel comfortable and not rushed. They communicate and pay attention to others, which increases the trust levels. A great way to spend more time with others in the organization is by attending employee events—socials, picnics, employee award programs. Your presence at these functions, as well as your absence, is always noted.

Manage perceptions. Perception is more important than reality because people will believe only what they imagine to be true rather than believe the actual truth. As a people-oriented leader, your job is to steer others' ways of thinking. Responding to others with "you should have known why I did that" or "you should understand why I take that position on that issue" is never enough to explain your decision. Always offer the most truthful, plausible explanation so that no one is left imagining any scenarios. Put yourself in your staff's mindset and think about how you would react if something unbecoming, such as the firing of a good employee, occurred.

Recognize others. Some leaders try to enhance their own positions and skills by demonstrating the inferiority of those who work for them and others around them. Strong, people-oriented leaders behave in the opposite manner—they *highlight* the skills and achievements of others, particularly their own staff members.

1. Listen very carefully to what others are saying—suggestion, feedback, criticism. Listening before responding will deflect your attention because you are concentrating on what is being said to you. You may still be angry at what you heard, but you will be more informed and better prepared to respond appropriately.
2. Remain open-minded to alternatives. Although your personal paradigm insists that you disagree, you must fight the urge to derail others' suggestions quickly. Reflecting first, instead of raging at the first opportunity, averts your attention and slows your reaction time.
3. Change your mindset and attitude. Meetings are often the breeding ground for heated arguments and unnecessary comments. Therefore, do not prepare for battle before the meeting because you will do battle if you do. Instead, prepare to respond to negativity, not battle with negativity.
4. Count to ten. If the prior suggestions do not work, simply counting may buy you time.

They understand that leaders today are more often measured by the successes of those on their teams. Therefore, the more recognition the team members receive, the more recognition given to the team leader.

Manage and channel emotions appropriately. Many leaders create problems for themselves by losing their tempers and showing the negative side of their personalities. Although everyone needs to vent, leaders must be careful not to lose control at the work place because uncontrolled emotions render them unprofessional, ineffective, helpless, and often feared.

Managing your moods is also necessary. Although moods can be positive or negative, moodiness is always coupled by a stigma—that it stems from poor mental health, which may or may not be true. If given a choice, some followers would probably prefer a constantly angry leader to a moody one because no guesswork is involved with the former. Leaders with good people skills show enthusiasm in their voices and in their body expressions when praising others. When serious difficulties occur, their tone reflects the mood of the situation.

Smile and be courteous. Many leaders would deem this suggestion trite; however, stories abound in executive search circles about executives who frequently fail to focus on the basics of strong visual courtesy. Zig Ziglar, a very successful sales trainer and author, is well known for teaching and coaching executives in this area. Many of his books reference the power of a smile.

Leaders with good people skills maintain good eye contact, without glaring, with whomever they are speaking. They practice body language that invites feedback and implies warmth and friendliness. They create an atmosphere of trust in which others can discuss issues with them and not worry about repercussions.

Focus on the needs of followers. "Take care of them and they will take of you" is a phrase that echoes the most basic way of developing and maintaining strong interpersonal connections. If you do not appreciate being disregarded, you simply cannot ignore your followers.

> Good leadership accommodates the needs and values of those who need to be led.
>
> Peter R. Scholtes[4]

Display compassion. Mutual understanding is the key to this. In the book *Reinventing Leadership,* co-author and former Avis CEO Robert Townsend recounts his experience with requiring all of his senior managers (including himself) to go through the Avis rental agent training school.[5] Although resisted by many of the senior managers, the experiment allowed Townsend to create a renewed spirit of support for Avis, which helped it through its struggling times, and to become a symbol of the modern CEO. Historically, many Catholic hospitals have maintained high employee morale and commitment. Those who have worked in these organizations will attest to the influence of the nuns in instilling compassion and concern for people.

Eliminate "put down" behavior. Yelling, angry outbursts, ignoring others, insulting others, putting them down are all inappropriate. Leaders who are secure with their position, status, and influence do not disparage, belittle, or discredit others and their subordinates. Employees who are the subject of ridicule and disrespect cannot be loyal and effective followers.

Exhibit optimism. One CEO opined, "One of the most powerful emotions is hope, and I try each day to instill it throughout my organization." Leaders with good people skills are eternal optimists because they cannot afford to be otherwise. Optimism encourages projects that appear doomed from the start, invigorates languishing suggestions or decisions, and rallies support and action.

Represent people who cannot represent themselves. The massive upheaval in the healthcare industry in recent years has taken a serious toll on workers. The past few years have brought large-scale staff downsizing or displacement and major reorganization. At times like these, employees must feel and know that their leaders are representing them. Leaders must be sensitive to the work lives of the employees who care and serve our patients.

CONCLUSION

Leadership is about building and maintaining relationships. The effectiveness of managing personal interactions is tied to how much leaders care about being with and working with others. Many years ago, the chair of a health administration graduate

> Despair means no choice, no options. Hope always provides options, always provides some glimmer of, 'Yes, we can do it.' That's what leaders have to communicate and embody and express in action.
>
> Warren Bennis and Robert Townsend[6]

> Optimism, like hope, does not mean simply waiting for good things to happen; it means acting in ways that create positive futures.
>
> James Kouzes and Barry Posner[7]

program warned me: "If you want to thrive in this business, you really have to love working with and around people. If you don't have a passion for that, go into another field." I cannot say it better.

*   *   *

SELF-EVALUATION QUESTIONS

- What does "people are our greatest asset" mean to me?
- Have I ever put other people down?
- Has anyone ever described me as a "people person?" Was this a source of pride for me?
- Has anyone ever described me as a good listener?

Chapter Seven

SERVANT LEADERSHIP

A new moral principle is emerging which holds that the
only authority deserving one's allegiance is that which is
freely and knowingly granted by the led to the leader in
response to, and in proportion to, the clearly evident servant stature of the leader.

Robert K. Greenleaf[1]

T HE HEALTHCARE INDUSTRY WAS established with
a simple, altruistic purpose: to serve the public. Therefore, its leaders must subscribe to the same edict by becoming "servant" to the needs of her/his organization and its
constituents. Servant leadership is the offspring value of willingness to serve others. It is not merely a trendy practice borne
by the end of the century's wave of political correctness or a
clichéd intonation of "following to lead"; instead, it is a skill

that delivers desired outcomes, boosts morale, strengthens the organizational structure, and yields support for the leader.

A servant leader is marked by the following characteristics:

(1) Focuses on the mission of the organization.
(2) Eschews selfish behavior and pursuit of personal ambition and biases.
(3) Sincerely respects all people.
(4) Realizes that the contributions of others are what enable the organization to fulfill its mission.
(5) Helps, encourages, and counsels followers to hone their skills and become better at their positions because doing so brings the organization closer to its goals.

Servant leaders give their skills, heart, time, and resources to improve their organizations and communities, and to set an example for others, as one CEO has done: "I gave each executive in the organization a small rock and a small ceramic monkey to place on their desks. The purpose is for them to be always mindful of what they need to do—keep the rocks and barriers out of the way so your staff can do their jobs. And if the staff can do their jobs, they won't put inappropriate monkeys on your back."

OPERATIONALIZE THE CONCEPT

The following are guides on how you, as a leader, can hone your servant skills.

Share information. Sharing information with peers and subordinates opens communication pathways through which ideas travel. Also, not hoarding information, or providing information only on a need-to-know basis, signifies the leader's trust and respect for others, disinclination to manipulate others or use the information in a power struggle, openness to suggestions, and willingness to help others understand the intricacies of the organization.

Listen intently. Author Robert Greenleaf suggests that "only a true natural servant automatically responds to any problem by listening first."[2] Listening is the paramount skill in developing solutions. Effective leaders are known for having intense listening skills, being open, and not making quick judgments.

Delegate authority. Leaders who delegate do not do so to establish subordinates or to boost their feeling of involvement, but to increase productivity. Delegation bonds people because it encourages teamwork, especially during times of crisis—although delegating is often hard during crises. Although many leaders tend to take the reins when problems arise, keeping the entire staff involved builds trust and develops camaraderie. In a crisis situation, leaders must closely coach staff but must not exclude them from involvement.

Support continuing education. All employees can benefit from continuing education to enhance their professional or vocational skills, which consequently improves their job marketability. Servant leaders must not only apportion organizational funds to finance educational pursuits for staff or seminars and programs that staff can participate in, but also must provide coaching. Some leaders provide "teaching moments," which are occasions when they help their staff understand the process involved in certain organizational events or issues that demand analysis and decision making.

Ensure successes for staff. Structured objectives and work assignments will help staff reach their goals and complete their assignments. Servant leaders must provide coaching if needed, but should allow staff freedom to work toward their objectives. In doing so, the staff gains mastery of their jobs and greater enjoyment from their work. Leaders who do this provide their followers with increasing confidence, skills, and feeling of accomplishments. Much like good parents with their children, these leaders will take great pride in seeing the successes of their staff. In essence, this exemplifies the Lao Tzu saying that successful leaders have followers who say "we did this ourselves."

Develop succession planning. In a battle, the sudden demise of a platoon leader can result in dangerous, if not fatal, consequences for the troop if no one assumes the leadership position. Military training places a strong emphasis on leadership succession. The same principle, albeit less traumatic, applies to healthcare organizations. Leaders must fully prepare others in an event that a succession is necessary. Servant leaders realize the importance of bench strength.

Maintain a helpful spirit and attitude. Servant leaders anticipate the needs of others and provide help and support when needed. Hence, employees and staff are not afraid to ask for help and clarification.

The greater the degree to which the vision is shared by employees and addresses their deepest aspirations, the greater the likelihood the leader will be seen as charismatic.

Jay Conger[3]

Lead by vision. A servant leader is a visionary and enlists others' help and expertise in achieving a vision. The logic is if others are invested in creating the vision, they are more likely to own it, be proud of it, and achieve it.

Demonstrate empathy. Servant leaders are empathetic to their staff because they are aware of the intricacies and difficulties of their work and often help out to alleviate stress. If they do not understand, they seek to understand so that they can better relate to the challenges—a feat that shows that they care and want to be involved.

Recognize and praise others. Servant leaders are acutely aware that people need recognition and praise for their accomplishments. They frequently interact with followers by expressing appreciation for the work being done. Simple practices carry great weight. Buying pizza when the credit and collection staff met their monthly numbers was just one way a successful CFO kept his staff enthused.

Provide performance feedback. Staff members also need feedback on their performance. Performance evaluation and appraisal systems are just a few ways to provide meaningful, unbiased feedback. Instead of dreading the evaluation sessions, servant leaders look forward to discussing performance and celebrating accomplishments. To be effective, a performance evaluation session will:

- focus mostly on the accomplishment of measurable objectives, which were developed during the prior evaluation session;
- look toward future performance and not dwell on the past;
- contain few, if any, surprises; and
- be developmental in nature.

Demonstrate connectedness. Servant leaders are not aloof or detached from their staff. History abounds with examples of leaders who achieved their successes by serving "in the trenches with the troops." Leaders who serve maintain close ongoing relationships with their staff and stay abreast of issues that may affect staff. Being connected requires dedication such as setting time aside to get out into departments and work areas. Leaders who spend all of their time in their offices become isolated from the organization. Several CEOs have developed programs such as "Walk in My Shoes" where the CEO actually goes to various departments and works alongside the staff. This program is usually better received than the traditional "white glove" military-type visits that some executives conduct.

CONCLUSION

Picture an organization in which everybody—leaders and non-leaders—performs every activity to serve someone else. The idea is if people feel served, chances are they will model that serving behavior throughout the organization. As a result, service to patients will be enhanced and the organization will be more successful.

*   *   *

SELF-EVALUATION QUESTIONS

- Why am I in the leadership position I hold?
- What is my leadership style? Does it place a heavy emphasis on controlling others?
- Does the idea of serving others make me think that I am a weak leader?

Chapter Eight

INITIATIVE TO MAKE CHANGE

"Our current success is the best reason to change things."

Iwao Isomura, Toyota's Chief of Personnel[1]

O NE OF THE MOST FUNDAMENTAL values that differentiate effective leaders from average leaders is the desire to make a difference. This value impels effective leaders, also known as "change makers," to become high achievers—constantly seeking out flaws and implementing positive change to improve their organizations in part and society as a whole. Those who grew up in scouting will no doubt remember the creed "leave a campsite in better condition than you found it." Change makers have internalized this creed—they

67

go a step further so that those who currently occupy the "camp-site" are happy and those who arrive later are impressed.

CHARACTERISTICS OF A CHANGE MAKER

In the 1960s, motivational theorist David McClelland posited that individuals who are high achievers are likely to be goal oriented and uphold high standards of performance. These individuals are most likely to move into leadership positions because they can operate well despite the stress and demands of the job—hard work and extra effort—and burgeon with every goal accomplished.[2]

Change makers are organizational participants who possess "restless discontent." These are leaders who, by the nature of their positions, must participate in processes with which they disagree until they can initiate change. The discontent stems from observing that the organization is ineffective or stagnant— muddling through poor management and operation. Ironically, the same discontent becomes the impetus for progress. One CEO called this discontent the "ability to sense opportunities." For many leaders, the desire to bring about change becomes a calling—a primary reason to exist professionally. Discontent peels away as change makers point to areas that need attention and garner support and buy-in from others in the organization. The continuous quality improvement initiative (CQI) is a product of the change maker's value. Some of the key principles of CQI are to:

- establish goals that are focused on improvement;
- develop systems and processes that will enhance out-comes;
- develop measures; and
- celebrate successes and make additional efforts toward further improvement.

OPERATIONALIZE THE CONCEPT

In flight school, pilots are taught how to maneuver their planes with the guidance of merely their instrument panel. This technique is important because it teaches pilots to remain capable of flying safely despite the hindrances that may surround them— thick fog, utter darkness, raging storms, or other conditions that impair visibility. However, new pilots tend to pay the most attention to one particular gauge on the panel—the altimeter— because it illustrates the position and location of the plane on the horizon. Although the altimeter is very important, the other measures tend to get overlooked, and this is when trouble ensues.

No analogy to leadership is more fitting than this instrument flight example. All healthcare leaders—new or seasoned—often mistakenly focus on only one measure—the financial meter— to determine the condition of the entire organization. The concept of the balanced scorecard, much like instrument flying, trains leaders to track all factors within the organization to guide them through difficult situations. (For more information on the balance scorecard, read *The Balanced Scorecard* by Robert S. Kaplan and David P. Norton.[3]) Leaders must be taught the same flight principles: (1) how to remain capable despite the disabling conditions thrown at them, and (2) how to look at all the measures. The following exemplify these principles.

Be objective-driven and progress-oriented. Change makers are passionate about setting objectives, both personal and organizational, because they help measure their own effectiveness. Unfortunately, some leaders today fail to measure the effectiveness of their work, processes, or outcomes. They perform responsibilities that are vaguely defined and they establish goals that are ambiguous. Standards are not clearly spelled out and as a result, determining progress with any precision becomes difficult.

A well-balanced scorecard also addresses determinants of success and survival, as well as measuring their status, enabling the organization to keep track of how its market position, customer perceptions, employee attitudes, quality processes, and innovations affect its performance. This helps the organization track and manage long-term as well as short-term success and survival.

Scott
MacStravic[4]

69

Lack of precision not only frustrates attempts to measure organizational performance but also harms the ability of the employees to get "on board" with the vision and direction that the leadership prescribes.

The best goals are made SMART—Specific, Measurable, Attainable, Results-Oriented, and Time-Bounded.[5] SMART, which is explained in the book *Credibility: How Leaders Gain and Lose It, Why People Demand It*, goals provide exact headings for the organization. All constituents of the organization naturally prefer this to a surprise, uncharted trip. SMART goals also allow organizations to focus simultaneously on the present—celebrate accomplishments as they occur—and the future—work on long-term goals.

Perhaps some leaders avoid developing explicit objectives because they are afraid of failing or prefer the comfort of ambiguity. However, change makers focus proudly on specific performance measurement. They work hard to get others to shape their vision with measurements so that change can be tracked. They constantly have their eye on all of the "gauges" that show them where they have been and where they are going.

Demonstrate courage. Change makers actually enjoy facing problems and are not afraid of taking risks—they risk over-identifying areas to improve rather than miss anything at all. Change does not scare them but becomes the norm in their leadership style.

Tom Peters, "father" of the excellence movement and a well-known management consultant, has argued in a number of public presentations over the past several years that many healthcare leaders lack the courage to make changes. Peters writes, "If you can't point to something specific that's being done differently from the way it was done when you came to work this morning, you have not 'lived,' for all intents and purposes."[6] He finds that in other industries, although mistakes are often made, significant progress occurs because leaders constantly try new

> Maintaining an unrelenting focus on people, performance, and change, however, demands courage. When the mechanistic organization gives way to the profoundly human challenge of broad-based, behavior-driven change, managers can no longer rely on traditional sources of authority or the power of decisions.
>
> Douglas K. Smith[7]

initiatives. Although Peters does not theorize why he finds health-care to be risk averse, I can think of one reason: the clinical side of the healthcare environment is intolerant of mistakes, which carries over to the business management side.

Celebrate accomplishments. People enjoy celebration. Effective leaders understand the need to occasionally pause and reflect upon progress that has been made. A celebration not only embodies the joy, relief, and pride of the accomplishment, it also resounds the gratitude leaders have for staff who were instrumental in the progress. People who are able to see that their efforts have made a difference and are appreciated are likely to repeat their performance in the future and feel empowered. Empowerment is a strong motivation because it makes people feel in control and valued.

One executive turned negative morale into positive by organizing a monthly "Breakfast of Champions" recognition program for its employees. Individuals and departments who made progress toward goals were recognized at the luncheon in which boxes of Wheaties were given as tokens of appreciation.

Develop a method of solving problems. Rather than a haphazard way of approaching organizational problems, change makers develop very specific methods to approaching and solving problems, which include:

(1) Confronting issues head on
(2) Identifying problems
(3) Defining and describing problems with a degree of explicitness
(4) Developing measurements to provide a baseline for future comparison
(5) Describing the negative aspects of the problems and identifying trade-offs
(6) Generating and weighing alternative approaches

> An effective vision integrates into the organization's purpose and into the employee's job a sense of contribution to themselves, to an industry, or to society. This sense of worthiness and influence can lead to greater commitment, enthusiasm, and the motivation to work harder.
>
> Jay A. Conger[8]

71

(7) Selecting an approach and developing measures for progress

(8) Implementing the approach

(9) Measuring progress and trying other solutions, if necessary

Do not accept the status quo; move toward continuous improvement. Long ago someone half jokingly suggested to me that status quo is Latin for "the mess we are in." Change makers realize that even in smooth-running operations, improvement is still necessary. They also realize that a state of equilibrium is a fictitious state; therefore, they engage in a relentless pursuit of improvement.

Seek additional responsibility. In their quest for progress, change makers continuously look for areas to expand and refine. For CEOs, this means expanding the outreaches of their organizations and establishing new services and/or managing other lines of business. Although some have suggested that integration and additional responsibilities primarily feed the egos of senior leaders, logic also dictates that they can enhance performance and service. For other executives, this means seeking ways to increase organizational accomplishments, such as actively participating in task forces and study groups and volunteering for new assignments.

Be passionate about benchmarking and networking. Change makers keep abreast of what other progressive organizations are doing by (1) interacting frequently with their leaders to compare solutions and ideas; (2) visiting their sites to scope out new technology, initiatives, or practices; and (3) frequently attending conferences and workshops. In addition, change makers are competitive. They continuously seek measurements to compare their success with other leading organizations, and they focus on the quantitative side of progress, especially on how others are doing. In contrast, leaders who seldom get out of their organizations lose their creative spark and lessen their perspectives in decision making and performance improvements.

Develop strong change-management skills. Today, one of the most requested attributes of effective leaders is the ability to manage—and bring about—change and its components including:

- Identifying the need for change based on the organizational vision and creating a sense of urgency to make the change
- Enlisting the support of others, particularly at the grass roots level
- Continuing to relate the change to the vision
- Utilizing a methodology in change (as detailed above in the problem-solving approach)
- Ensuring small wins and successes initially
- Celebrating wins and successes
- Imbedding the change within the culture of the organization

Build progress, not temples. For some leaders, wanting to make a change is fueled by an inappropriate desire to gain personal fame. While some personal recognition is appropriate and necessary, an organization's accomplishment is always a team effort and should never be mistaken as a one-person platform for prestige. When leaders take all the glory and stack points to win buildings named after them, their motives are questioned and followers tire of their incessant self-adulation and arrogance.

CONCLUSION

Accomplishments and improvements should be the primary *raison d'être* for leaders and should be the hallmark of service that people will remember long after the leader's tenure is over.

Neither objective, however, can exist without the leader's motivation, or the value of wanting to make a change. This value is the ultimate measure of the success, failure, or mediocrity of any organization.

* * *

SELF-EVALUATION QUESTIONS

- What have I accomplished that would become my hallmark of service?
- If I were to leave my organization suddenly, how would I be missed? Have I left a "mark" in the organizations in which I've worked?
- Flood lines along riverbanks indicate the height the water reached. If I used this parallel to measure my achievement, how high is my flood line?

Chapter Nine

COMMITMENT

...the more one's authority and breadth of responsibilities increase, the more control there should be over one's own time and commitments.... The head of an organization of any size quickly discovers that the great majority of his or her time must be closely related to that organization.

Ted W. Engstrom and Edward R. Dayton[1]

L EADERSHIP IS A DEMANDING master. It yields not to time. It bends not to excuses. It takes no vacations. It accepts only commitment. Commitment is a value that measures the leader's dedication to her/his profession. Because commitment binds people to their work, it generates from them a strong work ethic, loyalty, pride, productivity, ownership, and even joy.

Figure 9.1 lists definitions of commitment by several health-care executives. Note that some of the definitions equate leadership to a sport and compare commitment to the competitiveness and drive inherent in athletes. This is because many leaders view their positions as an athletic event. They prepare themselves physically, mentally, emotionally, and spiritually to face the challenges, competitors, and the stress. The stress becomes the adrenaline pump that inspires them to give the highest level of performance. As in sports, some leaders simultaneously act as "players" and "coaches" — inspiring others to do well by setting an example. Many leaders act as coaches and cheerleaders — motivating others to "get in the game" or "give 100 percent." Indeed, some of the more popular motivational speakers at leadership conferences are coaches, such as Lou Holtz, Joe Paterno, and Tom Landry, as well as athletes who talk about the personal sacrifices they made to reach their teams' goals.

OPERATIONALIZE THE CONCEPT

Maintain your commitment to your organization by following these simple steps.

Stay focused on clear and simple visions. Even during the most intense times, committed leaders always stay focused on their end goals. Their visions and goals serve as lighthouses in the darkest of storms and their commitment is tied to their drive to move onward. The visions and goals are not complex or hard to understand; they serve as an inspiration to others and create a clear direction for movement.

Maintain balance. Leaders who "live to work" lose perspective and burn out; therefore, they become ineffective — much like an athlete loses a competition when she/he fails to rest, trains too much, and overexerts. Workaholics place excessive demands on their staff and have unreasonable expectations. As a result, morale at the workplace is low; too many mistakes are made; distrust is prevalent; productivity is poor; and, most importantly, employees are constantly stressed out, fearful, and difficult to

FIGURE 9.1
Healthcare
Leaders' Definition
of Commitment

Commitment is...

"...getting the job done. You face all the hurdles and finish the race."

"...an attitude of excitement about any problem. Being committed means that you have the chance to fix it."

"...having a solemn covenant that you will do whatever it takes to fulfill the mission of your organization."

"...the old story of the chicken and the pig. The chicken gave eggs but the pig gave his life. That is true commitment. In some ways, I feel as though I have done the same for the healthcare organizations I have worked for."

"...giving your all because any race worth running is a race worth winning."

retain and manage. Employees are often happiest and more productive when these workaholic bosses are not in the office. Ways to avoid losing this balance include:

(1) Constant evaluation of the use of time. Many meetings are often unnecessary, so before you attend or host one, ask yourself: What will we discuss in the meeting? Do I have to be in the meeting? Can we accomplish the goal of the meeting without holding a meeting? What alternatives do I have? If I don't have to attend, what else could I accomplish?

(2) Constant prioritization of work and personal matters. First, write two comprehensive lists of what needs to be done inside and out of the office. Second, categorize both lists into Urgent (U), Important (I), or Can Wait (CW). Third, because many things can be urgent at the same time, number the list according to importance. A written list not only

reminds you with a visual aide, it also decreases
your stress because you feel more in control.

(3) Regular downtime. Executives should spend a block
of time—at least two to three hours a week—away
from all interruptions; they should spend one day or
two away from the office at least every four to six
months. This downtime allows you to check out of
the pressures of the job and regroup.

(4) Flexibility. Do not let the calendar rule you. But if
you find not following a schedule difficult, allow
extra time between appointments to accommodate
surprises.

Get a hobby. Healthcare is not an easy field to work in. The
massive changes occurring in the industry have pushed many
healthcare executives to the limit. Many admit to being fatigued,
tapped out, and wanting to change careers. This is why developing and maintaining interests that have absolutely no ties to
your job is imperative.

Introducing yourself to new undertakings removes you—even
for the weekends—from the mindset you are accustomed to having. Hobbies—no matter what you choose—present you with
creative problems that demand out-of-the-box solutions, which
enhance your thought processes and your judgment and give
you a different perspective. The most committed leaders have
outside pursuits. They regularly get away from their work to re-
charge their batteries and to rest. This gives them a renewed
vigor and helps them return to work with a regenerated commitment and energy level. Keep in mind also that a hobby may
simply be spending time with family and friends.

Show initiative. The greatest proof of someone's commitment
is when she/he takes initiative. Initiative is a personal drive to
chart a direction with no outside encouragement or command.
Some healthcare leaders define it as:

> Monitoring energy levels also means saving enough energy for nonwork-related activities. This is particularly challenging for today's health care executives, who find an unlimited number of demands of their time and feel compelled to respond to as many demands as possible.
>
> Austin Ross[2]

78

"Doing more than is required—going the extra mile."

"Actively seeking out issues and problems."

"Being proactive not reactive."

"Engaging in positive thinking."

"Not being a minimalist."

"Avoiding the negativity of blaming others and acting like a victim of circumstances."

Only by taking the initiative can you follow your own course, as the Spanish poet A. Machado writes: "Wanderer, there is no path. You lay a path in walking."

Be prepared to sacrifice. Author John C. Maxwell wrote: "Sacrifice is a constant in leadership. It is an ongoing process, not a one-time payment."[3] The healthcare industry is filled with seasoned leaders who frequently tell individuals new to the industry: "you must be prepared to pay your dues." This means that movement up the ladder toward greater responsibility requires giving up certain things, especially time.

"Make every workday Friday." This was a framed sign on the wall of a physician executive. According to him, the story behind it is: "When I was a resident, I was constantly struck by how excited hospital employees became on Fridays. Their whole attitude was positive. I saw their vigor and energy and how they approached their work. But, come Monday, well, that was a different story. After pondering this for many years, I came to the conclusion that it was only an attitude. And an attitude can be self-directed. So I had this sign made and framed to convey that attitude to others."

Although some critics say that positive thinking and attitude are fleeting and therefore ineffective, motivational speakers who espouse this virtue continue to fill seminars and meetings. Practically all—from Zig Ziglar to Stephen Covey to Colin Powell—convey one central message: work is attitude-driven.

Smile. So many executives today are under such stress that their faces reflect pained grimaces. Leaders with great interpersonal skills know that body language and facial cues send powerful signals. Commitment is often reflected in the facial expression. People want to know their leaders are highly committed, and one simple but powerful way that they gauge this is by the expressions on their faces.

Delegate. Delegation is one of the more basic skills taught at any management course, but it is one of the most overlooked and underpracticed. If you consider the typical turnover of power when a senior leader leaves the organization, you will get an idea of the concept. When new CEOs take the reign, they move much of the decision making up to their level. They do this to orient themselves about the organization, evaluate the decision-making of their subordinates, and begin to make their own mark on the organization. But in doing so, they fail to delegate responsibility to others; therefore, others are not given the opportunity to use their judgment or be part of the decision-making process. The cycle continues as new CEOs arrive.

Delegation is even more overlooked in times of organizational stress and trouble. When a crisis occurs, decisions are more closely monitored by the higher and highest levels of leadership. Ultimately, these CEOs get so overwhelmed and stressed out that mistakes become even more likely.

Continue to improve personal and time management skills. Effective leaders are always in control of their office and their personal lives because they know how to balance the two by being organized. Their files are systematic; their activities well planned and scheduled; their calendar well followed. They use the tools available to them that can help personal management—planners, computer organizers, e-mails, and other communication devices. They include their assistants in planning their schedules and provide them with insight into the plans and issues of the organization.

CONCLUSION

To committed leaders, work is not drudgery or toil; instead, it is a place where they find great satisfaction. In his well-known book, *The Seven Habits of Highly Effective People,* Stephen Covey lists being proactive as the first habit. According to Covey, being proactive is a function of commitment and work ethic.[4] Now, imagine an organization teeming with proactive workers and leaders, then realize that your organization can become one, too. As the saying quips: "Practice makes perfect."

✳   ✳   ✳

SELF-EVALUATION QUESTIONS

- Why am I doing what I am doing? Do I enjoy it?
- What does commitment mean to me?
- Do I feel that I am paying a price for the work I do? Is the price I am paying worth the rewards I perceive that I am receiving?
- We often hear people who have worked for many years talk about how they "paid their dues." What does this mean to me?
- If staff within my organization were asked to describe my facial expressions, what would they say?

- To what degree am I organized? Do I regularly run behind schedule? Do I keep a "to-do" list—and do I accomplish most of it?
- Consider the following quote from Jon R. Katzenbach and Douglas K. Smith. To what extent do I bring a personal level of commitment and working energy to the team table?

Teams work hard and enthusiastically. They also play hard and enthusiastically. No one has to ask them to put in extra time; they just do it. No one has to remind them not to delegate jobs to others; again, they just do the work themselves. To outsiders, the energy and enthusiasm levels inside teams are unmistakable and even seductive.[5]

Chapter Ten

EMOTIONAL INTELLIGENCE

Your first and foremost job as a leader is to take charge of your own energy and then to orchestrate the energy of those around you.

Peter Drucker[1]

I saw how the inability to manage emotions and communicate effectively often led to unresolved and repetitive conflicts among staff, low morale, and diminished productivity.

Hendrie Weisinger[2]

EMOTIONAL INTELLIGENCE IS a value that keeps leaders respected, admired, emulated, and followed. Why? Because emotionally intelligent leaders constantly better themselves to better serve others; they are self-aware, confident, enthusiastic, and energetic; they keep a positive attitude and teach—and encourage—others its value; they are motivated by improvements and changes; and they manage their emotions—positive or negative—appropriately to retain their dignity and to set an example.

Emotional intelligence comprises energy and maturity. Energy, which is sometimes referred to as the spark or zeal for life, refers to the liveliness with which leaders approach their work and from which they derive their stamina. It keeps leaders fresh and motivated through difficulties when others are ready to give up. Maturity refers to refinement, social graces, tact, ability to grow and change, and the knowledge to interpret signals given to us by others. It is the attribute that reminds leaders to apologize, to express gratitude, to harbor no ill will, to empathize, to have a sense of humor, and to respect others. Maturity keeps leaders composed and poised during times of distress, and wise during times of pressure. Although maturity is often associated with old age, it can be learned at a younger age.

> Emotional competence is particularly central to leadership.... Interpersonal ineptitude in leaders lowers everyone's performance: It wastes time, creates acrimony, corrodes motivation and commitment, builds hostility and apathy.
>
> Daniel Goleman[3]

Although emotionally intelligent leaders manage their emotions, they do not *lack* emotion. In fact, they may often show lots of emotions—optimism when situations are bad or confidence at times of defeat. The logic behind managing emotions is simple: People who work with leaders need to know how these leaders feel in order to follow their values and visions. Flat leaders, those leaders with little or no emotion, get those kinds of results—flat. They are not inspirational and they have difficulty convincing followers to follow. On the other hand, leaders who are passionate and display appropriate feelings are often able to keep followers enthused and eager to take on difficult challenges. The appropriate orchestration of emotions may be one of the best indicators of emotional intelligence.

OPERATIONALIZE THE CONCEPT

In the book *Emotional Intelligence at Work*, author Hendrie Weisinger sets out the following steps to improving emotional intelligence[4]:

(1)   Develop high self-esteem.
(2)   Manage your emotions.

(3) Motivate yourself.
(4) Develop effective command skills.
(5) Develop interpersonal expertise.
(6) Help others help themselves.

The main ingredient in these steps, according to Weisinger, is self-awareness. Leaders who are self-aware develop self-esteem, which is a universal panacea for negativity. Leaders with self-esteem are:

- willing (and even anticipatory) to accept constructive criticism;
- not defensive;
- supportive of those around them;
- assertive but not aggressive;
- confident in their ability to make change;
- win-win motivated;
- rarely hostile, overbearing, or impatient; and
- take charge individuals.

Leaders who are not self-aware misinterpret events or comments by others, throw tantrums or act out, and are unable to discern logic from the events that occur around them. They passively react to circumstances rather than proactively take charge of the situation. Unfortunately, many executives do not even realize how others perceive them because they have spent so much time away from their constituents that they have become insulated and out of touch. Despite their intentions, U.S. presidents lose touch with the country because they rely solely on poll results and counsel from senior advisors who are also insulated from the public. As a result, their reality becomes distorted, they lose their edge, and their emotional intelligence dulls. Although not to the same degree as U.S. presidents, many healthcare executives find themselves in similar circumstances. Without maintaining a vigilant guard against becoming isolated, they can begin to lose emotional intelligence by this separation from the mainstream of their organizations.

Leaders must develop strong feedback mechanisms and constantly assess themselves to avoid the pitfalls related to not being self-aware. The following are principles that can enhance emotional intelligence.

Develop feedback mechanisms. Emotionally intelligent leaders are self-aware because they welcome assessment tools, such as 360-degree feedback or other people's perception, that lay out delicate issues that if left not discussed can be deleterious to the entire organization. They relish the chance to receive ratings from their peers and subordinates because they are confident enough to not feel threatened. Leaders best able to develop strong feedback are those who:

- Are comfortable with themselves and relatively self-assured about their skills, goals, and visions.
- Practice intensive and reflective listening. They show a genuine interest in what is being said and allow the other person to lead the discussion. They are not known for constant interruptions.
- Do not threaten or intimidate others. They are open and approachable and do not allow the trappings of power to curb personal messages that others may give them.
- Are not always in a hurry. Leaders who portray a constant busy attitude signal to others that they do not have time for any information unless it is very critical.

The Emotional Intelligence Questionnaire (see Appendix A) is a tool that leaders can use to obtain direct feedback from others. To ensure comprehensive feedback, six people, from all levels of the organization, who work directly with or know the person being assessed should participate. To ensure confidentiality of the feedback, identification of the participants should not be revealed and participants should be discouraged from discussing their comments with others. Results should be collated by a third party—a neutral party—who will report the feedback to the person being evaluated.

Know your intentions. Be aware of your personal direction—know what it is that you want to do and accomplish. It is amazing how many individuals possess little sense of *personal* direction. This is often true of individuals who get caught up in the busyness of organization activities. They may be very effective in developing *organizational* goals and objectives and tracking progress toward them. Yet they fail to focus on their personal goals. They respond to the environment. Emotionally intelligent leaders know their long-term and short-term personal goals and seek organizations that provide them with the chance to achieve them. In other words, the organization's mission must synchronize with the leader's personal mission so that both entities can benefit from their union. For example, an individual who wants to work in a large complex environment cannot fit in a freestanding rural hospital or those who are mission-driven may not fit well in a for-profit system.

Emotionally intelligent leaders frequently take stock of where they have been and what they have accomplished. Some weigh their options by occasionally interviewing for other jobs even when they are not looking because it allows them to reflect on other opportunities and compare their skills and accomplishments with current standards. For others who are not as attuned to their intentions, the interview process can be intense and can cause unnecessary angst.

Make time for self-reflection. Most members of religious orders and some lay persons often take religious retreats. These are planned getaways, which last for a few days to a week, that focus on intense introspection. Although these retreats are intended to reconnect the participant to her/his original aspirations, some people go a step further: they reflect on their own strengths and weaknesses and seek ways to fit them into their own organizational style. One nun admitted to designing a succession plan while on a retreat.

Get a coach, a confidant, or mentor. Executive coaching has become one of the fastest growing areas of consulting. Executives in all industries are realizing the benefits of having neutral advisors—who work on a retained basis—who can provide relevant feedback on behavior, leadership style, and understanding and managing perceptions. Many emotionally intelligent leaders, even seasoned ones, have a coach with whom they can discuss private details of their jobs and from whom they seek counsel. A coach can help you continually clarify your intentions and help you create a clearer vision of your directions. Visit several coaching web sites on the Internet to gain a broader understanding, such as www.coachfederation.org, www.coachnet.com, www.coach.net, and www.stephenxavier.com.

Manage your emotions. Executives often reach points in their careers where they begin to get lax in controlling their emotions. They may become increasingly frustrated by the pressure and challenges and forget to temper their emotions in front of others. Over time, this frustration can often lead to a higher level of destructive anger and emotional outbursts. At first, the outbursts usually occur outside of the workplace but later they surface increasingly on the job. One search consultant admitted that he likes to play golf with clients to observe their ability to control their emotions. Another frequent sign of poor emotional control is labeling individuals by calling them "names." This may occur during direct confrontations or the name-calling may occur when they are not around. Neither case is appropriate.

In the book, *Emotional Intelligence at Work*, author Hendrie Weisinger notes that physiological changes—or arousal—occur when people start feeling anger, nervousness, or excitement.[5] These changes include heart palpitations, perspiration, and rapid respiration. By being aware of these physiological signals, we can slow down our reaction time.

Learn to deal with setbacks. Leaders respond to setbacks differently. Because they are more optimistic, emotionally intelligent leaders respond more positively. They often welcome the challenges that surface during setbacks. Some leaders take a mental or physical break from the activity and return with a sense of renewed commitment, while others use setbacks as personal challenges to do better the next time. One CEO's professional philosophy was: "If you get knocked down, you get up and try again." She actually had a small laminated card in her wallet that said:

You will get knocked down at times;
You will taste dirt occasionally;
But it is through this process that
You will better enjoy the return to the air above.

Manage your energy level. Strong leaders find that when they become too tired, they lose their effectiveness, and they become short-tempered and unpleasant to be with. Those around them try to find times to communicate with them when they are not so unpredictable with their emotions. Effective leaders learn early in their careers that a good balance of rest, ample sleep, and regular exercise can give them an edge.

CONCLUSION

Emotional intelligence is so important now because leaders do not live and work in a "command and control" environment anymore. In the past, respect often came with position; however, leaders today have to earn it. They do this in part by demonstrating control over their emotions and maintaining their composure during times of adversity. They "keep their heads." Having the energy and maturity to manage an organization is a feat on its own; managing emotion as a stepstool to effectiveness is a work of art.

*   *   *

SELF-EVALUATION QUESTIONS

- How isolated have I become from direct personal feedback?
- How well do I know myself?
- Would others say that I am plagued by frequent bouts of emotional inconsistency (outbursts of anger, hostility, and antagonism)?
- To what extent do I manage my emotions?

PART III

Team Values

Chapter Eleven

COOPERATION AND SHARING

Self-centered people believe the key lies in them, in their techniques, in doing 'their thing' to others.

Stephen R. Covey[1]

OO MANY MEETINGS TODAY have a hypnotizing *show-and-tell* style: One by one attendees of the meeting *tell* the others about her/his project, and *show*—with some illustration (PowerPoint overheads and hand-outs perhaps)—how the project is scheduled and coordinated. Of course, questions are volleyed and answers are proposed, but often very little attention is given to identifying—or solving—problems that could arise, or have arisen, from the projects. Often no one asks in detail how—or why—the project is going to be done, and few others volunteer their help. At the end of these meetings, people file out only interested in their own projects and still removed from others'. Consequently, when successes or failures happen they become an individual's accomplishment or sorrow, rather than a team celebration or setback.

Although the healthcare industry prides itself for emphasizing individual authority and accountability, it should also support and encourage team dynamics because building teams means strengthening efficiencies. Team effort enhances:

- Coordination and reduces bureaucracy. When people are assigned a specific function, overlapping responsibilities, duplication of duties, and red tape become past practices.
- Involvement and support. Because everyone works together toward a common goal, the focus shifts from receiving personal glory and recognition to supporting the team's objectives and valuing the contributions of others. "That's not my job" is replaced by "It's all of our jobs."
- General oversight and reduces problems that "fall through the cracks." Everyone is involved in making sure that nothing is overlooked or undermined.
- Joys of celebrations. One of the reasons that sports bind people is everyone enjoys watching the exhilaration of team victories. An accomplishment is always grander when more people share and enjoy it because it represents each person's own contribution of hard work, sacrifices, and dedication.
- Creativity. When more people are involved various perspectives and new ideas are generated and better results are achieved.

Teams are predestined for failure without the fundamental values of teamwork—sharing and cooperating. Team members must be willing to sacrifice some of their individuality to benefit the entire team.

OPERATIONALIZE THE CONCEPT

Strengthen your team with the following strategies.

Build the team right in the first place. Most CEOs who come into an organization rebuild all or at least part of their executive team. They do this for two reasons: (1) to establish their "mark" on the organization; and (2) to assemble a team of people who espouse similar values. Most executives who are tapped to become part of the new team are "excited" about the opportunity. Often, this excitement translates to wanting to share and cooperate. When recruiting, leaders must consider people who believe in the concept of teams. Evaluate prospective members with the following guidelines.

(1) Ask prospects to recount an actual situation in which they worked with a team and by doing so developed a solution that was much better than their own. Listen carefully for the candidate's inclination—or disinclination—toward teamwork and behavior.

(2) Ask prospects to recount an actual situation in which they had problems working with teams. Ask them how they handled their frustration.

(3) Ask prospects to describe a situation in which team efforts do *not* work very well.

(4) Ask prospects the values that drive effective team interaction (see Chapter 15).

(5) Administer a validated personality assessment, such as the Hogan Personality Inventory, to assess the prospect's personality and leadership style and how they would support effective team interaction.

(6) Do targeted referencing by asking specific questions on team behavior. Ask references to describe how

the prospect gets along with fellow team members. Ask for examples of how the prospect argues or debates issues during team sessions. A good idea is to ask the extent to which the prospect "plays politics" among fellow team members.

Discuss the value and values of the team. All team members should discuss their individual expectations, evaluate their personal worth to the team, and establish the values that govern team interactions and behavior. Doing so improves relationships and cooperation. Because team members are often so busy with their own daily activities, they often fail to invest necessary time to fully grow and develop as a team. In the landmark 1998 study *The War for Talent*, McKinsey & Company reported that most effective companies have leadership teams that have candid and above-board debates during meetings.[2] Members of these teams prefer an atmosphere that encourages spirited discussion and admit that better decisions evolve out of this process.

Under an autocratic CEO, the concept of discussing the importance of a team is a farce. Teams under this type of leadership exist merely to fill the conventional office. Members of these teams neither know how to, nor want to, partake in the decision making. As a result, these members are not aware of their roles and importance. Of course, the underlying problem in this scenario is the leader; however, the team can be salvaged by a new leader. The new leader can ingrain the values of teamwork into the minds of the members with constant discussion and team exercises.

Demonstrate the value of "teaming." Team leaders must involve all team members in setting achievable short-term goals. The achievement of these goals demonstrates the team's value and contribution to the improvement of the organization. This is one area in which an effective CEO can demonstrate the value of teaming by bringing tough issues to the group and really allowing the team to solve them as a group. CEOs too often keep many of their more difficult problems to themselves or within a smaller subset of the managing team.

Determine the purpose of the team. Unfortunately many leadership teams do not know why they exist. When asked, most respond with: "We share information" or "We discuss strategy." Some even say (perhaps mistakenly): "We run the organization." A clear purpose—and awareness of it—outlines the direction toward which the team is headed. This clarity eliminates prospective or existing team members whose intentions are vague, inappropriate, or do not fit.

Several years ago, I led a senior management team retreat. Before the retreat, I met individually with team members to ask them the following questions.

- What are the primary reasons for the *existence* of this senior management team?
- What are the primary reasons for the *meetings* of this senior management team?
- Does the *content of the meetings* support the primary reason for the existence of the team?

The responses were varied, but most members indicated that their primary reason for existence was to "collectively lead the organization." Later in the retreat, many revealed that their meetings primarily served as show-and-tell sessions, instead of being the collective interaction that they all prefer. This revelation segued into an in-depth discussion about the need to (1) shape and follow a clear purpose and (2) restructure meeting patterns. The team decided to meet every other week solely to discuss strategy and to meet weekly to discuss day-to-day operations. As a result of this discussion, the majority of the team remains intact

> The best teams invest a tremendous amount of time and effort exploring, shaping, and agreeing on a purpose that belongs to them both collectively and individually. In fact, real teams never stop this 'purposing' activity because of its value in clarifying implications for members.
>
> Jon R.
> Katzenbach
> and Douglas
> K. Smith[3]

today. The members report being closer and managing conflicts more effectively.

Engage in team-building exercises. Any exercise that confirms the collective strength and assesses the dynamics of the team and aids in the interaction among team members is beneficial. Common team activities range from simple personality-assessment tools, such as the Myers-Briggs Type Indicator and Hogan Personality Inventory, to extensive physical undertakings, such as Outward Bound. These activities are fun and provide a more relaxed environment for members.

Confront relationship issues. Deal directly with the negative situations. Develop a team style that makes tough person-to-person confrontation appropriate and acceptable. While at times this requires intervention by the team leader, who can impose sanctions, the team itself will often engage in policing behaviors and doling out punishment including isolating disruptive members.

Developing a team code of conduct is a great team-building exercise because it requires participation, cooperation, and careful input from all members. In essence, the members outline the rules that will both protect and monitor their behavior and interactions.

Several senior leadership teams have done this during retreats and have found the exercise extremely valuable. Figure 11.1 is an example of a team code of conduct, which has been adopted by many healthcare organizations and is currently used by a midwestern health system.

Challenge the boundaries that exist. Traditional hierarchical organizations build boundaries that create rigidity and inflexibility including the following, which are adapted from *Touchstones: Ten New Ideas Revolutionizing Business* by William A. Band[4]:

FIGURE 11.1
Team Conduct
Expectations

- Each of us has a right to her/his own opinion and has the right to state it. Each of us expects that others will carefully and respectfully listen to our opinion and seriously consider it before rejecting it.
- Although our CEO has the authority to make unilateral decisions, he will engage all of us in giving input in as many issues as possible. We respect his right to "some days count the votes and some days weigh the votes."
- We recognize that some decisions are better made with subsets of our team. However, except in unusual situations, we agree that these decisions will not be finalized until the entire team is notified.
- Each of us has the right to campaign for our issues outside of team meetings. However, we agree to tell the team that this campaigning has been done.
- Mystery, intrigue, and politics are fatal diseases. We will strive for openness, honesty, and tact.

- Boundaries of authority—who is in charge of what?
- Boundaries of task—who does what?
- Boundaries of politics—what is our payoff?
- Boundaries of identity—who are we as a group?

The faster these boundaries come down, the faster cooperation will take place, as one CEO told his executive team: "I expect all of you to work together as though you had authority for the entire organization. Leave your claims of functional turf at the door."

CONCLUSION

Decision making, problem solving, and brainstorming are activities that predicate a leader's daily existence. These activities are most effective when executed with others and when various perspectives are considered. But the others in this scenario must be people who subscribe to and practice the inherent characteristics of teamwork — coordination and sharing.

* * *

SELF-EVALUATION QUESTIONS

- Has my team ever discussed the reason for its existence? Its purpose?
- Do team members truly believe in the value of teaming? or the value of team deliberations?
- Does my team regularly participate in team building activities?

Chapter Twelve

COHESIVENESS AND
COLLABORATION

Cohesiveness 'is the sum of forces that attract members
to a group, provide resistance to leaving it, and motivate
them to be highly active in it.'

Richard L. Hughes, Robert C. Ginnett,
and Gordon J. Curphy[1]

ANY LEADERSHIP TEAMS in healthcare strive to capture the "entrepreneurial spirit" that teams in successful businesses possess. The entrepreneurial spirit—or cohesiveness—is a mindset that congeals teams and cheers them on through conception, development, and marketing of new products and services. Unfortunately, this spirit is impermanent and permeable by old-fashioned jealousy and selfish tendencies. When a business expands its operation, it naturally adds new members to its existing team, which is a logical progression but potentially destructive to the cohesiveness of the team. What subsequently occurs between the original

101

members and the newcomers are quarrels over decisions, dissension over leadership issues, and decreased support for the common goal. In essence, although cohesiveness increases productivity, morale, and camaraderie, it does not prevent schism from occurring. Leadership teams, then, should strive to capture not only this spirit but the intricacies of maintaining it.

Collaboration pulls together divided parties to work toward a mutually accepted goal. It transcends traditional compromise in that no exchange of services is necessary to achieve the preferred outcomes of both parties; it only demands equal input and dedication to the cause. Most importantly, collaboration often results in conflict resolution. Conflicting parties typically react by adopting one of the following approaches:

- Avoid the conflict altogether
- Give in or accommodate the other party
- Compete—drive toward the classic win/lose scenario
- Compromise or strike a deal that gives something to both parties
- Collaborate—drive toward a win/win scenario

Consider the last three approaches. Competition is never an appropriate response because it amplifies the damage and makes it irreversible. Historically, compromise has been recommended, but it leaves both parties only partially satisfied. In compromise, both parties tend to "save" favors, supposedly owed to them, so that they can "cash in" during future conflicts. Note that if neither party anticipates future dealings with one another, then a compromise is usually a better approach than collaboration. Conversely, if the parties continue their relationship and expect further dispute, then collaboration is the only responsible solution. This is the case with senior leadership teams. Cohesiveness begets collaboration and collaboration begets cohesiveness. Although one can exist without the other, one cannot be as effective without the other.

As illustrated by the entrepreneurial-spirit analogy, team cohesiveness has its downsides, including:

(1) *Low performance norms.* Performance norms are expected of each member of the team. These norms dictate the quality and quantity of work—how vigorous, how effective, how productive, what goals were achieved, and what contributions were tendered. Because these norms are usually unwritten and solely enforced by the team members, they tend to get overlooked when the team is highly cohesive and cooperative. As a result, the performance norms lower and productivity decreases. Why the contradiction? The reason is twofold: in cohesive teams, (1) highly competent members pick up the slack for members who have less-than-par abilities; therefore, those who need skill enhancement are pardoned and often disregarded; and (2) competent members have become complacent and too polite to subject poor performers to constructive criticisms.

(2) *Proliferation of "groupthink."* Groupthink occurs when team members become so enveloped in unanimous thinking that they lose their individual objectivity. As a result, new and creative thoughts are blocked off, objections are stifled, and concurrence becomes the standard. Instead of pursuing the goals of the organization as a whole, keeping the solidarity of the team becomes the team's main purpose. Figure 12.1 lists symptoms of groupthink.

(3) *Low tolerance for new members.* Teams that are peopled by "founding members" who abide by tradition and are comfortable with its identity and its mission do not kindly welcome change—particularly in membership. New members are often viewed as disruptive outsiders and detrimental to the cohesiveness.

FIGURE 12.1
Symptoms of
Groupthink

Groupthink is:

- *An illusion of invulnerability*, which leads to unwarranted optimism and excessive risk taking by the group.
- *Unquestioned assumption of the group's morality* and, therefore, an absence of reflection on the ethical consequences of group action.
- *Collective rationalization* to discount negative information or warnings.
- *Stereotypes of the opposition* as evil, weak, or stupid.
- *Self-censorship* by group members from expressing ideas that deviate from the group consensus due to doubts about their validity or importance.
- *An illusion of unanimity* such that greater consensus is perceived than really exists.
- *Direct pressure on dissenting members*, which reinforces the norm that disagreement represents disloyalty to the group.
- *Mind guards* who protect the group from adverse information.

Source: Reprinted from *Leadership: Enhancing the Lesson of Experience, Third Edition* by Richard L. Hughes, Robert C. Ginnett, and Gordon J. Curphy. 1999. Originally adapted from *Groupthink* by Irving L. Janis, 1982. New York: Irwin/McGraw-Hill.

(4) *Team goals that take precedence over organizational goals.* A highly cohesive leadership teams is fanatical about the welfare of its members. Some teams have been known to reduce clinical and support staff and still maintain excessive administrative support staff. Some organizations still pay executive bonuses even during difficult financial years.

OPERATIONALIZE THE CONCEPT

As we have established, cohesiveness is an important key to collaboration, but its disadvantages must be seriously considered because they sometimes outweigh the advantages. The following are methods that will help you build a cohesive team without building disadvantages.

Minimize selfish behavior. Selfishness is a contagious disease. To prevent it from spreading, you must disinfect yourself first. Demonstrate that you are working on behalf of others' interests, not just on your own. If your team members suspect that you are using them or their people, cohesiveness will decline. CEOs and team leaders are responsible for confronting members who display selfish motives and do not contribute to the well-being of the team. Appropriate team behavior must be verbally addressed, possibly at a retreat, and must be written (see discussion about code of conduct in Chapter 11).

Decrease the size of the team. The acquisitions of new service lines and corporate entities of many healthcare systems have greatly widened the reach of leadership teams and expanded their size. This growth has split the focus of the team—some members attend to external functions, while some concentrate on internal operations. As a result, the commonality that used to be so ubiquitous has been replaced by conflict of interest, as the following sentiments from CEOs attest. "We have had more turf battles and less cooperation since our executive council has grown in size and we have picked up additional business lines," admits one CEO. Another stated, "As I saw our senior team grow from 11 members to 18, I saw us lose our camaraderie and team spirit."

Although decreasing team size is difficult because it affects the status—and egos—of existing members, it must be done to preserve cohesiveness. One approach is to divide operations and strategy executives into two teams. Another approach is to hold the meetings of the larger team less frequently, and convene a smaller team more frequently. Some teams seize the opportunity to rebuild or resize when executive turnover occurs; this way, no egos will be harmed and no status is affected.

Dedicate time to get to know one another. Spending time does not imply holding longer meetings to "share" because that can be very counterproductive. What I do suggest is much more fun: socialize with your members! Seize every opportunity presented to you including work parties, lunch periods, before or after meetings, or celebratory gatherings. These interactions not only create a personal bond between you and them, it also communicates a much powerful message: you are interested in them not only as a co-worker but as a person. Consider the following examples practiced by some successful CEOs. One CEO takes her senior team off-location every fourth Friday for a morning "retreat." They cover business during the morning meeting, adjourn for lunch at 11:30, then spend the afternoon just talking about nonwork-related matters. Another CEO takes her team to a local country club the day after their monthly board meetings to enjoy each other's company and catch up. Yet another CEO holds a weekly lunch session that includes no formal agenda but allows informal and often nonwork interactions among the group.

Minimize the influence of cliques. Unfortunately, cliques are not confined to junior high school and they are prevalent in all organizations. The larger the organization, the larger the teams, and the larger the problem of cliques. Cliques are detrimental to any team because they represent dissent and selfishness. Because being in a clique can signal disagreement with the team as a whole, clique members may tend to be less cooperative, more ambitious, and more manipulative. Clique members can influence the team's decisions—whether negatively or positively—because they have solidarity, which is thatched together by each member's personal designs.

The impact of cliques can be minimized several ways:

(1)   Occasionally recognize the cliques' existence during team meetings, as one CEO does each time:

"Well, I know that the operations people (or other identified subteam) have already come to a conclusion on this matter," he begins, "so can we hear from you a synopsis of the discussions that took place before our meeting today?" By making them publicly known, the cliques realize that the team is aware and will not cower to their caprice.

(2) Directly confront them privately. The CEO, the team leader, or even peers can address the difficulty that cliques can create, the negativity that they can engender, and the anonymity that they can spread. This confrontational method clearly communicates to cliques that their intentions will not be tolerated.

(3) Assign conflicting members to the same task forces wherein they can work toward the same goal. The purpose here is to improve relations and spread out the expertise and knowledge that members withhold only for her/his own clique.

(4) Discuss the existence of cliques with the whole team and how this can harm team performance. This is often best done under the expert guidance of a facilitator.

Ensure that the team understands why they exist. As discussed in previous chapters, all team members must be on the same vehicle that will take them forward. Frequently clarify your goals, your purpose, and expectations. Discuss them with the team and make changes, if necessary. Strive for 100 percent commitment and support by making everyone on the team part of the development of the goals. Nothing inspires cohesiveness more than personal involvement.

Ensure that all team members are equal. Imbalance of power produces divisiveness, which is the mother of cliques. This phenomenon is often caused by the actions of the CEO or team leader. The CEO or team leader must treat all members equally before, during, and after team meetings, inside or outside the meeting room. Personal relationships must be managed to avoid creating the perception—real or imagined—that different levels of influence exist.

Discuss and assign roles to each team member. A specific role in a leadership team heightens the sense of belonging and importance of any member. Roles include being a team spirit leader, devil's advocate, team conscience, team historian, "mom," "dad," or meeting room organizer. Although seemingly simplistic, these roles give the assigned member a reason for attending and actively participating. Some teams use team-building sessions to discuss roles that can be assigned.

Consider a heavier emphasis on team compensation. If the compensation structure of an organization is designed to recognize and reward individual performance, then team behavior will receive less attention. As a result, team members will think and act more selfishly because they are only compensated for their individual merits. While the purview of this book is not compensation, attention must be given to the fact that it affects team cohesiveness, hence its effectiveness.

Manage team meetings to ensure equality of interaction. The golden rules of meetings are (1) dedicate ample time for discussion of key issues and (2) dedicate ample time for every team member to provide input. Many examples of these principles exist, including the following. To prevent turf battles, one CEO required his team to wear a generalist operations hat during debate on organizational issues. To get members involved, one CEO calls on team members who have not spoken or taken an active role in discussions, while another assigns members a specific point of view—either devil's advocate or proponent—

to take during a debate. To elicit a wider response, some CEOs use Nominal Group Technique (NGT) or other team discussion tools.

Rally the team against an outside threat. Competition, acquisition, and downsizing are only three of the real-world pressures that organizations today face. Many CEOs have used these as outside threats to unite senior and middle management teams and medical staffs, to gain support, and to stretch and strengthen the muscles of cohesiveness and collaboration. A note of caution is appropriate here: too much attention spent watching the activities of a competitor can cause an organization to lose focus on its own core competencies.

CONCLUSION

Without cohesiveness and collaboration, the greatest victories in sports, the classic symphonies, the most successful peace pacts would never have existed. A healthcare leadership team that lacks these values cannot fulfill its many potentials nor be beneficial to itself, its organization, and its community.

*   *   *

SELF-EVALUATION QUESTIONS

- Why does my team meet? What do we accomplish when we meet?
- Would outside observers describe my team as cohesive?
- Has my team studied collaboration? Have we had training in conflict resolution?
- Consider the symptoms of groupthink listed earlier in this chapter. What symptoms do my team exhibit?

Chapter Thirteen

TRUST

An understanding of people and relationships requires an understanding of trust. Trust requires the coexistence of two converging beliefs. When I believe you are competent and that you care about me, I will trust you. Competency alone or caring by itself will not engender trust. Both are necessary.

Peter R. Scholtes[1]

TEAMS ARE UNIMAGINABLE without trust. Imagine convincing people whom you do not trust and who do not trust you to cooperate. Imagine sharing information with them. Imagine collaborating with them. Imagine asking them for help. If you can imagine any of these scenarios without feeling paranoid, doubtful, exhausted, desperate, exasperated, and doomed, then I salute you; please skip to the next chapter. If you cannot, please keep reading.

The first value that team members must learn is earning and giving trust. This is why the "can-I-trust-the-person-behind-me to-catch-me-when-I-fall-backward" exercise is so popular and so well used. Without trust, teams become mantels on which trophies for fierce competition, back stabbing, and hypocrisy are displayed (see Figure 13.1). But what is trust and how does it fit the purposes of the team?

The *Merriam Webster Collegiate Dictionary, Tenth Edition* defines trust as the "assured reliance on the character, ability, strength, or truth of someone or something."[2] In leadership teams, trust is each member's confidence in each other's capacity and resolve to uphold and work toward the team's vision. It is what allows one member to vote for another's untested, seemingly outlandish proposal. It is what makes members stand behind their leader in moments of great failure or scrutiny. Figure 13.2 discusses the essence of trust within team dynamics and Figure 13.3 enumerates and defines the essential components of trust.

The underlying motive for giving trust within the team is not as altruistic as one's esprit de corps, however. In teams, trust is given because of this supposition: what is put out is paid back. The mindset of each member is to continually show and have faith; provide support, assistance, information, and resources; and align with the team so that favors that potentially can help their individual causes may be returned. After all, a spot on the leadership team is a coveted position because of the individual rewards it presents to all its members. Trading services, products, or favors is modeled after the economics of bartering.

The primary purpose of bartering is to trade services or items that are equal in value to benefit the parties involved—one bushel of corn is not a fair trade for five acres of farmland. Similarly, team members who trade trust also expect certain parity. As the Peter Scholtes' quote submits, trust is dependent on competence and caring. Although this trust becomes a favor, it is not easily exchanged because members still have to prove to each other that they are capable, responsible, and care about the members' and the team's well-being. If members are worthy, the barter of trust is considered a success, becomes an implicit

FIGURE 13.1

Lack of trust among team members results in:

- information hogging;
- undermining;
- inappropriate competition for resources;
- side bar deals;
- lack of or inappropriate participation in team discussions or decisions;
- proliferation of power cliques;
- detrimental politics and games playing; and
- war and casualties.

FIGURE 13.2

Team members must:

- *Speak their feelings.* Trust cannot grow and develop when feelings are buried and team members do not completely know what each other thinks about ideas and issues.
- *Maintain confidentiality.* Many of the discussions that take place within a team setting must be kept confidential.
- *Actively support the team.* Trust can be quickly destroyed if team members talk negatively about others outside the team setting.
- *Embrace openness.* An open and candid environment develops trust. Hiding information is very detrimental to trust.
- *Practice due process.* Due process is a legal term that means existence of a formal set of rules to hear concerns. Within the team setting, it means that all team members have the right to have their ideas and their objections heard fairly.

FIGURE 13.3

Recent research has identified five dimensions that underlie the concept of trust:

- *Integrity:* Honesty and truthfulness.
- *Competence:* Technical and interpersonal knowledge and skills.
- *Consistency:* Reliability, predictability, and good judgement in handling situations.
- *Loyalty:* Willingness to protect and save face for a person.
- *Openness:* Willingness to share ideas and information freely.

Source: Reprinted from *Organizational Behavior, Eighth Edition* by Stephen P. Robbins. 1998. Upper Saddle River, NJ: Prentice Hall.

norm, and is practiced by more members. This trade is not only beneficial for the individuals but for the team. When members become unwilling or cease to trade trust, a "depression" occurs, which is similar to an economic depression that results from low output of, but high demand for, products. This depression prohibits cooperation and multiplies poor decisions.

OPERATIONALIZE THE CONCEPT

The following suggested methods guide you in enhancing trust levels among your leadership team peers and subordinates.

Openly discuss the *quid pro quo* of team dynamics. To ensure that the team fully understands the bartering model, discuss it and emphasize its functions and advantages. Weave it into trust-building exercises and practice it.

Trust in a relationship generally develops gradually over time through the course of personal interaction. Taking some kind of risk in relation to the other person and feeling you weren't injured (emotionally or physically) in the process is what moves trust to new levels.

James Kouzes
and Barry Posner[3]

Recognize that earning trust takes a long time. Trust does not occur overnight, which is a universal truth that impatient leaders just have to accept. Because the healthcare industry is often in a state of flux, its leadership team is also often in flux. This type of environment does not foster the growth of trust.

Develop consistent behavior. Trust, in some respect, is about predictability. Do not convey contradictory messages or say conflicting statements. For example, many CEOs prescribe openness to senior staff, but do not include them in decision making and unveil strategic plans only when they are ready to be implemented. Some CEOs often tell their staff "Come and see me anytime you have a problem," but wall themselves in impenetrable executive suites. When staff members ask to see them, they are often told to follow the chain of command. Other CEOs are guilty of inconsistent moods—feeling up one day and down the following. These swings of temperament can be very destructive to the development of trust.

Although being paradoxical is poetic and intellectual, it confuses others and sends them a totally different impression: you're capricious, indecisive, and untrustworthy. "Practice what you preach" is more than just a well-known adage; as a leader, you must live by this long-standing creed.

Drive out fear. In his book, *Beyond the Wall of Resistance*, author Rick Maurer writes that "the opposite of trust is fear." He believes that the absence of trust starts a pattern of fear that escalates to resistance to change.[4] As resistance increases, people become polarized and trust decreases further. Although difficult to perish, fear has no function on your team. Create a nonthreatening environment in which your staff can freely discuss, suggest, criticize, and be truthful. Recognize their individual accomplishments and offer assistance when needed.

Develop an open style of leadership. Avoid creating an environment of secrecy because this is how rumors propagate. To dismiss suspicions and placate mysterious myths about leadership team meetings, one CEO regularly invites departmental managers and physicians to come. To encourage involvement, another team leader holds "Think Out Loud" meetings with her senior staff. These meetings take place off-site and have an open, brainstorming format so participants can relax and suspend—even for a few hours—their regular activities and thought processes. These meetings not only generate great ideas but also build trust.

Set an example. "You cannot please everybody all of the time," but you can bet that when you are the leader, everybody is always watching you. The concept here is not to please, although it is inevitable to try to do so, but to follow what you set out to do so at the end of the day nobody can accuse you of being hypocritical, being self-important, or being tyrannical. When I ask participants at my workshops to describe the characteristics that

excellent leaders with whom they have worked possess, the responses always include:

- Someone who doesn't keep you guessing because she
  plots out everything and follows it
- Someone with clear values. You know what he
  stands for
- Someone who is always willing to do what she asks you
  to do
- Someone who shows you the way and gets out of the way
  so you can do it on your own
- Someone who doesn't just give directives, but also
  pitches in
- Someone who is always there for you

By setting an example, you are also communicating that you
can be trusted because you are not afraid to do the duty yourself.

Practice candor. Candor is the sincerity and frankness of your
speech. It prevents you from lying, condescending, or exaggerating. People trust you more if you are not constantly fawning
over them or telling them what they want to hear. Practicing
candor, on the other hand, does not suggest being insensitive or
bullish. Ways to speak or confront someone frankly but con-
siderately include (1) retaining eye contact; (2) speaking with a
soft voice; (3) weaving sympathetic phrases or terms into your
soliloquy; (4) making the confrontation brief by stating only facts
not opinions that do not add merit to the charge and only hurt
the other party; and (5) allowing the other party to respond.

Retreats are optimal moments for candid discussions, as John
Kotter proposes in his book, *Leading Change*: "Most of the time
must be spent encouraging honest discussion about how individuals think and feel with regard to the organization, its problems

and opportunities. Communication channels between people are opened or strengthened. Mutual understanding is enlarged. Intellectual and social activities are designed to encourage the growth of trust."[5]

I have led several senior leadership team retreats that yielded no visible results because no team members were willing to directly address the issues. Although they often told me their concerns before the retreat, they became silent when all members of the team finally converged. To combat this, I started meeting with individual team members in advance of the retreat to discuss the merits of openness and to recruit each one of them to contribute to the discussion and speak their minds. I also occasionally bring written lists of concerns to the first session (but I always received permission from the team members first) so that we start from the same basis.

Learn and practice tact and diplomacy. Finesse does not cost anything but is worth a small fortune. However, like a battery, finesse is negatively and positively charged. While dealing with someone with decorum and courtesy is a plus it is also a minus because it prohibits confrontation needed to reveal underlying conflicts. For example, a cohesive leadership team that has been together for many years and has not argued over issues does not take kindly to confrontation. As I've suggested in Chapter 12, a cohesive team does not necessarily make a productive team because many of its members have grown complacent about issues, so it can use a little shake up once in a while. Having tact, however, saves you from being boorish when the duty of reorganizing is assigned to you.

Embrace and respect resistance to your ideas. When you ask for trust, you also ask for a certain amount of vulnerability. Expect criticism of your visions and ideas but be prepared to accept them and not take them personally, as one CEO described it: "If you want trust within your management group, you have to expect to get shot down sometimes. Then you get back up, thank the person who shot you, and move on."

Be accessible. Some senior leaders seem to "hide" in their offices because they are afraid of criticism and exposure. They require that all public meetings must be carefully orchestrated so surprises are either nonexistent or few, and they make sure that the order of events or agenda is highly predictable. You do not need me to tell you that people fear, hence mistrust, those who are constantly inaccessible or invisible. Put yourself in your staff's shoes and imagine how quickly they back pedal at the thought of your arrival. Then once you taste their fear, set aside time to reassure them that you are not someone to be feared—unless you enjoy intimidating others.

Do not take advantage of others. Although the bartering model may not seem to exemplify this concept—because it teaches you to seize the opportunity to serve yourself—it really does. The golden rule of bartering remains: you cannot trade a product or service that is not worthy or equal in value. If you follow this principle you cannot take advantage of others because you can take only what you are allowed to give.

Grant authority appropriately. As the CEO or team leader, you have the power to bestow decision-making capabilities on members of your team, so you must exercise extreme care and judgment. You cannot grant it because you favor someone or something, and you cannot grant it because you lack awareness. Create a climate in which all team members feel comfortable with providing expert assistance and input. Do not allow your meetings to become show-and-tell exchanges because when it reaches this level, you will remain unaware and your decision making will be futile.

> High-performance teams are characterized by high mutual trust among members. That is, members believe in the integrity, character, and ability of each other. But as you know from personal relationships, trust is fragile. It takes a long time to build, can be easily destroyed, and is hard to regain. Also, since trust begets trust and distrust begets distrust, maintaining trust requires careful attention by management.
>
> Stephen P. Robbins[8]

CONCLUSION

Evaluate your own teams against these guidelines:

- To what extent does each of us, as team members, believe in one another's abilities and competence?
- To what extent does each of us, as team members, believe in one another's inclinations and intentions?
- To what extent does each of us, as team members, believe in one another's integrity?
- To what extent does each of us, as team members, get along with one another?
- To what extent does each of us, as team members, truly share the same goals?
- To what extent does each of us, as team members, rely and depend on each other?
- To what extent does each of us, as team members, have confidence in the predictability of each other's motives and behavior?

Trust is a feeling that individuals have when they believe that they can share or confide in another person and can feel assured that the other person will not use that against them. It is the purest form of good will.

＊　＊　＊

SELF-EVALUATION QUESTIONS

- Is my leadership style marked by openness? Do others easily approach me?
- To what extent am I known as a good team player?
- To what extent is communication open within my team?

- To what extent are we candid and straightforward with one another?
- Do we support one another? Do we help and coach each other?
- Are we pleased with individuals within our group accomplishing things? Is appropriate credit given?

Chapter Fourteen

CONFLICT MANAGEMENT

An underlying aggressiveness drives all business imagina-
tions. It has content and direction. It also stimulates con-
troversy. People will disagree, particularly if the position
taken affects their own power and place. So leading with
substance requires maturity not only to tolerate others'
aggressiveness but also to direct it toward substantive
issues.

Abraham Zalesnik[1]

ONFLICT IS THE NATURAL byproduct of human
complexity and interaction. It is present everywhere,
even in seemingly uncomplicated tasks such as deciding what to order at a restaurant. The magnitude and accelera-
tion of a conflict are always dependent on the number of people
involved, which is why teams are a breeding ground for volatile
disagreements. Complex systems beget complex hierarchical
structures beget complex conflicts. As we have discussed, the

days of autocratic leadership are dwindling and are being succeeded by team-driven governance. Leaders progress in today's environment by becoming engineers of consent—opening up to others' suggestions and steering them to concur on a common goal—and managing the discord that may potentially arise.

Unfortunately, however, many CEOs continue to stifle conflict, fail to discuss and confront its genesis, and have not established a conflict-management guideline for the entire team. The reasons—or excuses—are varied: some CEOs see conflict as a disease that can destroy the cohesiveness of the team and impede its growth; some are too busy to engage in confrontation and resolution; some simply are afraid to grapple with a subject so menacing; and others are so confident in their abilities to handle a conflict that they handle it only on an as-it-happens basis, rather than establish a preventive plan of action.

The biggest irony is that team conflict is good because it:

- *Ends complacency.* Conflict turns members from being too satisfied with everything to being concerned about everything. Members start to question ingrained, inefficient processes, traditions, and decisions.
- *Initiates discussion.* Although discussion is scarce at the beginning of a conflict as parties strategize, it soon ignites as conflict deepens.
- *Steers action.* Whether or not the subsequent action is beneficial or feasible, conflict inspires action.
- *Demands participation.* Members who are otherwise inactive and silent become involved when conflicts exist because they tend to choose sides that best represent their views.

Although conflicts are inevitable, they are manageable. Teams who do not manage their conflicts are doomed to quick disintegration.

Management teams whose members challenge one another's thinking develop a more complete understanding of the choices, create a richer range of options, and ultimately make the kinds of effective decisions necessary in today's competitive environments.

Kathleen Eisenhardt, Jean Kahwajy, and L. J. Bourgeois III[2]

OPERATIONALIZE THE CONCEPT

Assume that you, as a leader or team member, are already convinced that conflict is a necessary evil, the next step you must learn is how to acknowledge and manage it if you cannot completely avoid it.

Discuss and adopt conflict-management guidelines. The first step toward conflict management is acknowledging that conflict inevitably occurs when intelligent, opinionated people converge. The second step is developing rules so if a conflict does occur, all members can debate, deliberate, and compromise accordingly. These guides should be reviewed regularly by all members of the team and new members must be informed of its existence. Figure 14.1 is an example of a conflict-management guideline.

Develop a common approach. Minimize conflict by discussing, and possibly adopting, a working style that can benefit all. For example, if the team's size makes quick, thoughtful decision making impossible, divide the team into several subteams or have every member volunteer for them. The subteams can be assigned a specific agenda for which its members are accountable.

Be careful with *directspeak* technique. *Directspeak* is the straightforward manner of communication without being insensitive. *Directspeak* does not work everywhere, but it thrives in team settings in which trust prevails because every member of these teams knows that confrontations are never meant to be personal attacks. CEOs or team leaders must be aware that some team members are uncomfortable with this technique, toe the line to avoid offending others, and are not active participants in debates. Conversely, some members are strong-willed and more

Teams must agree on how they will work together to accomplish their purpose and goals. Real team members always do equivalent amounts of real work beyond and between meetings where things are discussed and decided. Over time, a team's working approach incorporates a number of spoken or unspoken rules that govern contribution and membership.

Douglas K. Smith[3]

123

FIGURE 14. 1:
Conflict
Management
Guideline

1. Declare the conflict. Not all discussions during group interaction are conflict-oriented. When a struggle ensues, however, someone must inform everyone that a conflict has arisen so that proper procedures can be followed. Although this may sound trite, it can become a powerful tool for managing conflict appropriately.

2. Give reason for the conflict. Although disagreements and arguments are normal and necessary, they cannot be initiated out of caprice or malice. Strife, hostility, and animosity must still be avoided at all cost, but if they do surface the reason(s) must be stated.

3. Clarify the issues of conflict. A neutral group member or one who is not directly embroiled in the conflict must be elected to clarify contentions and interpret ambiguities. All members must actively participate in the dispute and specify in detail their issues. Although members are entitled to express their concerns based on their emotional ties, facts must govern the debate, not opinions.

4. Address one conflict at a time. To ensure appropriate and thoughtful consideration of all issues, only one issue at a time will be considered. Although many people tend to save their issues and raise them all during debates, it will not be allowed or tolerated. All members should address their concerns as they occur.

5. All members must participate. No party in the dispute will be allowed to "pull in their heads" during the conflict. All must give their opinion and not cower behind their given parties.

6. Be fair. Members must keep their weapons appropriate to the level of the fight. In other words, a member cannot keep attacking without giving the other a chance to retort and defend.

7. Declare that the conflict is over. All members must know that the debate has ended and an outcome has been reached. The outcome agreement should be specifically defined so that no confusion, which could escalate into another conflict, arise later.

verbal, which may intimidate the mild-spoken members. What results is another conflict: a personality conflict. One way to minimize personality conflict is to emphasize the greater good of the team or to focus on the goals during debate. When certain debates among his senior team become too fierce, one CEO jots down the goals of the debate on a flip chart to help the team focus on the issue and not on attacks.

Strengthen the team dynamic. One of the fundamental ways to build a stronger team is to revamp the compensation system. Team-based compensation maximizes the willingness of members to serve and stay because if team members were paid according to what they accomplish for the team, then they are more likely to believe in and work harder toward the goal. Another way to reinforce teams is by creating a culture in which members are accountable for the results of each decision and responsible for reaching the team's objective. Often the only way that this team culture or attitude can be created is when the CEO or team leader, who has the most power within the team, enforces it.

Teach and reiterate conflict-management approaches. In Chapter 12, I enumerated the five approaches—avoidance, collaboration, compromise, accommodation, and competition—to conflict. These approaches are typical in that they illustrate the sink-or-swim mindset of many teams.

Unfortunately, avoidance is always one of the first approaches, but it is valid only when the conflict is too minor to merit full-time consideration. When major conflicts are sidestepped, they will absolutely escalate in intensity and meaning. Although collaboration lasts longer and builds strong relationships among parties involved, it is seldom a practical response. The reason for this is that trust cannot be earned quickly so breaking down barriers and ambiguities is time consuming and does not fit the quick-solution pattern. Compromise is the most democratic and most satisfying approach because it works for both parties, but it is also the most overused. It also stalls decision making because too much consideration and not enough action are taken to satisfy everyone's demands. Accommodation is the most temporary and dangerous approach because it is based on giving and receiving favors. When members start "accommodating" or giving in to the demands of others, they do it not because of some heartfelt belief in the other member's causes but because they expect the favor back. This trading perpetuates distrust, bureaucracies, and fear. Competition, which is sometimes called "forcing," is the classic win/lose approach. The win column refers to some arguments won and the lose column refers to everything else. Competition serves only to create an environment in which members posture for authority and influence and misuse team meetings as personal battlefields. Perhaps the only time this approach is appropriate is when tough decisions have to be made and competing against each other will yield a faster, possibly more efficient result.

Identify and eliminate the antecedents of conflict. As does everything in the universe, conflict has a beginning and an end. And as with many things in the universe, the beginning and the end are controllable. The ideal end of conflict is a solution that not only suits everyone but is lasting. The ideal beginning is insight to know what will work and what will not. In the book, *Organizational Behavior*,[4] authors Robert Kreitner and Angelo Kinicki list the following warning signs:

- Incompatible personalities or values systems
- Overlapping or unclear job boundaries
- Competition for limited resources
- Inadequate communication
- Interdependent tasks (e.g., one person cannot complete

his or her assignment until others have competed their work)
- Organizational complexity (i.e., conflict tends to increase as the number of hierarchical layers and specialized tasks increase)
- Unreasonable or unclear policies, standards, or rules
- Unreasonable deadlines or extreme time pressure
- Collective decision making (i.e., the greater the number of people participating in a decision, the greater the potential for conflict)
- Decision making by consensus
- Unmet expectations (i.e., employees who have unrealistic expectations about job assignments, pay, or promotions are more prone to conflict)
- Unresolved or suppressed conflicts

CONCLUSION

As healthcare systems continue to become more intricate and as quick decision making becomes the norm, conflict can only keep pace and become as complex, or even more so. Although conflict can exist alone, it thrives within teams. To a strong team, it is a temporary foe but a permanent ally. To a weak team, it is a predator. What role does conflict play on your team?

*   *   *

SELF-EVALUATION QUESTIONS

- Has my team discussed methods for managing our conflicts? What are they?
- Has my team discussed our conflict-management styles? What are they?
- Do we have a CEO or team leader who does not allow

conflict to surface? If so, does the suppression drive the strife outside where the fighting is more political and harmful?

- Has my team moved toward decreasing uncertainty in our working environment to minimize conflict?

PART IV

Evaluation

Chapter Fifteen

EVALUATE YOUR TEAM MEMBERS

In the typical senior working group, individual roles and responsibilities are the primary focal points for performance
results. There is not incremental performance expectation
beyond that provided by individual executives working
within their formal areas of responsibility.

Jon R. Katzenbach and Douglas K. Smith[1]

HOW DOES YOUR LEADERSHIP team function? Is
the leadership role filled by a sole CEO or shared by
all members? How do you discuss and deliberate issues? Is everyone on the team accountable for the results, or are
members assigned particular responsibilities, or both? No matter what the set up of your team is, the main principle of this
book remains: you—as a leader and/or team member—must
subscribe to a set of values because they determine your current
effectiveness and future success.

A team's success is solely possible because of the dedication
and consistent hard work of its members; therefore, the best

quality indicators of any team are the values that its members adhere to. Evaluate your team members against the following values.

(1) **Skills.** The triumvirate of skills—technical, decision making, and interpersonal—is a necessity in a leadership team setting. Although each of these skills is essential and may gain a member entrance into the team, it cannot sustain the member for long. For example, if a member possesses astounding technical, or expert, training but lacks interpersonal skills, she/he may eschew daily interaction, may not contribute to the general camaraderie, or may alienate others who are less technically-oriented. Similarly, if a natural decision maker joins the team without adequate specialty training, her/his contributions may not be as worthwhile. Although these skills may not be advanced, members must have all three.

Ask yourself: Do we, as members, possess this triumvirate of skills?

(2) **Awareness.** Awareness is a golden value because it prevents confusion and expedites solutions. In an effective team, members know each other's specific function, especially the leadership structure. Although governance is shared and goals are mutually agreed upon by all members, each issue is overseen by a central person to discourage manipulation and negotiation for position and control. Each member is aware of who is responsible for issues, such as budget and clinical, and each member keeps abreast of current and future events of their teams.

Ask yourself: Are we fully aware of our roles and responsibilities, both formal and informal?

(3) **Participation.** The reason members are aware is that they value active participation. Members establish the team's roles and norms. Roles are expected behaviors of members who are in specific positions or who display specific personalities. For example, the role of the chief financial officer is that who is "frugal" because she/he is in expected to be financially practical. Nursing or human resources executives are traditionally placed in "caring" roles. Although inappropriate, stereotypical, and biased, some "sensitive" roles are given to female members, while "tough" roles are doled out to males. Norms, on the other hand, are acceptable behavior inside and outside team meetings. Some consultants term norms as "around-here *isms*" because all members must abide by these norms lest others criticize or even isolate them from the rest of the team.

Ask yourself: Do we participate in establishing our team's roles and norms? Do we understand them?

(4) **Cohesiveness.** Members value cohesiveness because they know that it eases the difficulty of working with other personalities, it reduces animosity and politics, and it increases the possibility of achieving the goal. One way of solidifying cohesiveness is by establishing traditions in which everyone can participate. For example, to discourage lateness, one leadership team purchased a piggy bank in which members deposit a $1 donation when they came to a meeting late. The money was contributed annually to the United Way. Members also know, however, that too much cohesiveness results in selfish team behavior and complacency.

Ask yourself: Are we cohesive? What traditions do we uphold?

(5) **Commonality.** Members value commonality, which is why they magnetize toward others who share their values, goals, commitment, and even backgrounds. Having a common thread lessens explanations and justifications and produces consistent, solid decisions.

Ask yourself: Do we have a common vision? Do we have other things in common?

(6) **Commitment.** Commitment conjoins people. When members are committed—especially to the team and its goals—they work harder, set aside their personal ambitions, support team efforts, avoid contention, and engage in team decision making. Although team commitment and personal commitment differ in that the latter revolves around the self, the end result of both is the same: success.

Ask yourself: How committed are we? Are we committed enough to become productive?

(7) **Communication.** Communication dictates the direction of any team. Without it, any team revolves in circles. With it, any team moves forward. Members espouse the power of interacting with others because it is the easiest road to the efficient exchange of ideas and the efficient resolution of conflicts. Effective communications should be frequent, open, candid, and accurate.

Ask yourself: How frequently do we communicate? Is there balance in the discussions and debates that take place?

(8) **Interdependence.** Interdependence is a value because it links all members by forcing them to depend on each other. As mentioned above, each
member has a triumvirate of skills that helps her/
him maneuver. However, no one member is highly
advanced in all three skills, which means that she/
he still requires assistance from other members.
Without interdependence, issues are only partly
considered, projects are only half-completed, and
conflicts are always fully pledged.

*Ask yourself: How interdependent are we? To what extent do we
rely on each other for support and input in decision making?*

(9) **Camaraderie.** Camaraderie humanizes people and
makes possible other values, including cohesiveness,
communication, interdependence, and participation. Members spend time together outside work or
the team setting, which allows them to discover
each other's similarities and dissimilarities. Although
having camaraderie is a benefit, too much of it can
translate to the formation of cliques within teams.

*Ask yourself: Are we personally compatible and have we devel-
oped camaraderie?*

(10) **High energy.** High energy is a value because it initiates action. Members with high energy are more
productive, creative, and supportive. Meetings become an anticipated event, rather than a chore.
Enhance your team's energy by:

- *Trying a new meeting location.* New locations
  waken and refresh interests because they create
  a new-beginning mindset. Many retreats are

effective solely because they take place in a different location.

- *Celebrating team and individual accomplishments.* Festivities always reverse moods positively, and good mood translates to high energy.
- *Inviting outsiders to present to the team.* Good presenters are trained to inspire and rally people to act.
- *Taking a break from routine.* Routine is energy draining, so break from it once in a while to invigorate your team and give them something to look forward to. The break does not need to be work-related, but it should be fun and meaningful. One CEO occasionally sends her team to visit patients. Another CEO arranges for occasional afternoon outings to the movies.

Ask yourself: Do we have high energy level? Do we have fun working together?

CONCLUSION

Constant evaluation allows you to predict the future of your team. Seize each opportunity for assessment. Strive to be closer to perfect. Ask each member of your team, you included, to answer the questions at the end of each team value above. Compare and contrast all the answers and discuss them.

*   *   *

SELF-EVALUATION QUESTION

- If I could change one thing about my team, what would it be? Have I shared that with my team?

> The best team experiences occur when you can really feel the energy of the team. It feels synergistic. It's exciting.
>
> Lisa Kimball and Amy Eunice[2]

Chapter Sixteen

EVALUATE YOUR SENIOR LEADERSHIP TEAM

All the empowered, teamed-up, self-directed, incentivized [sic], accountable, reengineered, and reinvented people you can muster cannot compensate for a dysfunctional system. When the system is functioning well, these other things are just foofaraw. When the system is not functioning well, these things are still only empty, meaningless twaddle.

Peter R. Scholtes[1]

A SENIOR LEADERSHIP TEAM is a complex wheel. Its hub is its basic structure—size, membership, hierarchical structure. Its spokes are the components that make possible its activities—roles and norms, protocols, objectives. Its rim is the outcome of its two primary activities—meetings (for purposes of coordinating) and decision making. Each of these elements contributes to the overall strength of the team. Just as you cannot judge the quality of a wheel by inspecting its rim alone, you cannot declare the team successful based solely on the usefulness of its processes and decisions.

TEAM STRUCTURE

SIZE

Teams that comprise 12 or more members are too large and those with a membership of four or fewer are too small to oversee the multifaceted functions of an organization. The book *Essentials of Organizational Behavior* suggests that seven is the ideal number.[2] Although we all would like to attain this ideal number, downsizing or upsizing to reach it is not realistic because so much depends on the expertise and strength of the existing members. Smaller teams make decisions faster because fewer people are involved to counter and question each issue. Members on smaller teams develop camaraderie, personal relationships, and trust faster and more deeply. On the other hand, larger teams boast more experts who contribute thorough suggestions and detailed facts to the decision-making process. However, as team size increases, two conflicts arise: team leaders become authoritative to establish order, and team meetings start veering from problem-solving forums to information-sharing stations.

Ask yourself: Is my team too large or too small? What are the advantages and disadvantages of re-sizing my team?

HIERARCHY

Although humility is the virtue that prevents people from brandishing about their accomplishments and forces them to say "titles don't mean anything to me," it is not the same virtue that commands them to be truthful. The importance of titles and status within the organization cannot be minimized. They are very important, especially to higher-ranked officers.

A title, or hierarchical status, is not merely a definer of responsibilities; it often plays a covert role in team efforts because it bears prestige and influence. Unfortunately, many leadership teams bestow titles, hence power, inappropriately to entice participation and recognize accomplishments. An imbalance of power occurs as a result, which makes skewed hierarchy possible: vps, Senior vps, and Executive vps occupy the same decision-making seat. As mentioned before, compensation or incentive awards can be used to recognize members without using titles as such.

Ask yourself: Do we recognize and respect the hierarchy on my team? Do we appropriately bestow titles?

MEMBERSHIP

Membership to or participation in leadership teams is very prestigious and is often perceived as a perquisite—a reward for holding a position within the organization—rather than a worthy, appropriate station. This perception is possibly culled from the disproportionate representation of departments or interests at leadership meetings. The following exemplify situations that illustrate this imbalance of influence.

- The public relations director is a member who is in charge of disseminating organizational information to all staff. This membership creates the perception that this individual is a higher-ranked manager than other departmental directors.
- The senior vp of patient care services and the vp of nursing are both members. Because both have nursing backgrounds, the perception that they may be partial to nursing issues seems true.
- Although not vps, the director of human resources and the chief information officer are members.

139

- The director of the medical staff regularly attends meetings, although the individual is not a member.

Membership and attendance must be supported by sensible and logical criteria, not merely a favoritism-like approach. Criteria for membership must consider:

- Candidate's position within the organization
- The position's importance and its contribution to the organizational diversity of the team
- The position's potential contribution to the overall goal of the team
- Candidate's expertise or training that can be beneficial to the team
- Other logical reason for membership

Ask yourself: How is membership on my team viewed? As a privilege? As a reward? As a form of recognition? Do my team meetings include invited guests? Are they regular attendees? What role do they play in the meetings? Does my team have established criteria for membership or participation?

TEAM ACTIVITIES

MEETINGS

All teams meet. Many would argue that without meetings goals could not be set or met. I recently surveyed a group of healthcare executives to determine how meetings eclipse their actual work time. The answers were astounding: some executives spend 60 percent of their work time attending meetings, while some admit to attending 90 percent of the time. In addition, many reveal that at least half of these meetings "waste" their time. The next time you sit in a poorly planned meeting, think of the wasted expense that is represented in the room in the form of salaries paid and think of the revenue-producing opportunities that could be waiting for you.

Necessity

Unfortunately, meetings have been so ingrained in all of us that we have become conditioned to facilitate and attend meetings without questioning their purpose or relevance. Nobody pauses to think about it anymore. Nobody dares to bow out. Nobody misses a next meeting despite the poor outcome of the last one. But this conditioning must end somewhere somehow because it is costing your organization much needed money, time, and energy. To determine the necessity of an upcoming meeting, simply do two things: (1) review your notes from the last gathering, and (2) ask if your participation is required. If you must go, then you at least know that your time will not be wasted and your input will be anticipated.

Ask yourself: Are my team meetings necessary? Are they regularly scheduled? Have I questioned their relevance?

Objectives, Agendas, and Necessary Materials

The necessity of a meeting depends solely on the objective. Objectives specify the purpose of the discussion. If meetings were called merely to share information, then all participants must know it ahead of time so that everyone can be prepared and everyone can get the opportunity to decide if attending is necessary.

One way of informing every member of meeting objectives is by utilizing an agenda. Agendas direct the course of the meeting by explicitly enumerating the issues that need to be discussed. Equipped with an agenda, team members can minimize digression and curb loquacious attendees from dominating the discussion.

Another way of communicating the objective of the meeting is by providing relevant material in advance. Fortunately, the protocol at many meetings now is that no item that requires preparatory material—financial statements, statistical report, proposals, etc.—can be discussed if material is not disseminated ahead of time. Teams that do not practice this protocol waste time with covering basic material and rehashing old information.

Ask yourself: What are our meetings' objectives? Does every member know them? Who determines the objectives? Do we follow an agenda? Who prepares it? Who controls it? Are our meetings fairly controlled to minimize sidebar conversations, multiple discussions, and other interruptions? Do we require preparatory material?

Roles and Norms

The *role* each member plays either in meetings or outside of them must meet the *norms* of the team (see Chapter 15 for further discussion on roles and norms). For example, if the CEO is the "chair," she/he must come prepared, come on time, come to stay, come to listen, come to participate, and come to ensure order during the meeting.

Ask yourself: What is my role and does it abide by the norms that my team has set? What types of roles and norms have my team established? Do we follow them closely? Do cliques or factions exist within my team? If so, do they have a different set of norms?

Time

Meetings are ravenous eaters of time. Flexible meetings are wasteful because they encourage too much deliberation and too little resolution. Although thoughtful discussions prevent risky undertakings, they are impractical in an environment pressured by constant change and quick fixes. The biggest time wasters are information-sharing meetings, which must not last longer than three hours. Although meetings in which strategies are developed and shaped must not have time limits, they should still be scheduled in advance and planned. Part of this planning is distributing a summary or minutes of the past meeting to refresh attendees. The minutes are also a great tool for initiating discussion.

Ask yourself: How long do our meetings last? Do we have a regularly scheduled, time-limited meeting, or is it often flexible? Who keeps minutes? How soon after meetings are they disseminated? Are they detailed or vague? Are they used by anyone?

Format

Generate creative ideas by changing your format from a passive-aggressive discussion to a participatory interaction that not only enhances your understanding of each other's responsibilities and expertise, but also displays your commonality and personal leanings.

(1) *Parking Lot.* Brilliant suggestions, questions, and solutions that are not directly relevant to the discussion often come up during meetings. Although some of these ideas are spontaneous and creative and some are thoughtful and detailed, they are hardly remembered, except perhaps by the people from whom they originated, in an agenda-driven meeting. Many teams, however, have begun to use a system called the "parking lot." The parking lot is a figurative term for the flip chart on which ideas are written or "parked" until the time they can be discussed and considered appropriately.

(2) *Multi-voting.* When there are too many issues on the agenda and all seem equally important,

multi-voting rescues the team by allowing each member to vote on which issue can stay and which can go. Each member is given a set number of votes. The issues list is posted on a flip chart so members know for which they are voting. Each member votes silently and confidentially to shield her/him from potential political ramification. The issues that receive high votes survive. This technique is very democratic and provides members who do not prefer to verbally argue a chance to be heard.

(3) *Affinity diagram.* Similar to multi-voting, this technique allows the team to organize a large number of ideas or issues. Each member is given sticky notes onto which she/he can jot down specific issues and general topics of concern. They then can group these sticky notes accordingly. This grouping or diagram ultimately guides the team in prioritizing and assigning responsibility.

(4) *Process mapping.* This technique literally maps out, on large paper that can be tacked on the wall, work processes. Process mapping is useful because it familiarizes all members to a certain method: its intricacies, responsible parties, outcome measures, etc. This map ultimately guides members when they make modifications to existing processes.

Ask yourself: Do we manage our meetings creatively? What is our typical format? Have we considered changing it?

Etiquette

Proper conduct in proper places is a universal human rule. Inappropriate behavior in team meetings is always unacceptable because it is disrespectful and unprofessional. Unfortunately, rudeness has become common place in many meetings. Consider the following meeting behavior and determine if either you or your colleagues have ever displayed any of them.

- Bringing paper work or reading materials to meetings in which a presentation or video will be presented—the idea here is to show up but "tune out" everything that seems to have no impact or relevance to the person
- Constantly stepping out during meetings to handle "more important" issues or crises
- Constantly stepping out during meetings for coffee or restroom breaks
- Not actively participating in the discussion but plotting to tackle the issue in a different forum
- Occasionally scheduling appointments that conflict with regularly scheduled team meetings
- Constantly interrupting, talking at the same time, dominating the discussion, complaining or arguing, and holding sidebar conversations
- Constantly arriving late

Ask yourself: Do members on my team work on or read other items during meetings? Do our meetings start on time? Are members on time? What are the sanctions if members are late? Is misbehavior accepted? How do we address and correct it?

Participation

All-member participation translates to all-member satisfaction. Every member must contribute to the team's goals because every member benefits from them. Conflicts of interests arise when only part of the team gets involved and not everyone is represented. Team leaders or fellow members must draw quiet members into the discussion by using techniques such as direct questions or nominal group technique (NGT). NGT's goal is to count and deliver each member's opinion; its process is as follows.

(1) A specific problem—usually complex and demanding numerous alternative approaches—is identified.
(2) Each team member writes down solutions.
(3) Solutions are shared with everyone. The team leader records them on a flip chart.
(4) Each solution is discussed, clarified, and evaluated by the entire team.
(5) A final list of solutions is compiled.
(6) Each member votes on the solutions based on her/his priorities.
(7) Each solution is ranked based on the number of votes.
(8) Final decision is determined based on the rankings.

Ask yourself: Is attendance required at our meetings? Do all members actively participate? What kind of tools do we use to encourage participation?

Conclusion

End the meeting right. Many meetings last so long that by the end, participants are so eager to leave that they fail to hear the last minutes of the discussion. The final minutes of any meeting should be the strongest because at this time the leader can rally support for the issues discussed and motivate the team to follow through. The team leader must conclude the meeting by providing a very short—a sentence or two—summary of each issue, without repeating all of the details, to remind everyone of what was covered.

Ask yourself: How do we end our meetings? Do our members leave exhausted and unmotivated? How can we remedy this?

DECISION MAKING

Many teams become proficient in avoiding decision making. They discuss issues over and over, but achieve neither solution nor compromise. Other teams fear the conflict that may result from their decisions, while others invite repercussions by making harsh decisions. No matter which category your team fits into, or does not fit into, you should consider the following questions when evaluating your decision-making structure.

- Do we have an identifiable methodology for decision making? Have we been trained in team decision making?
- Do we use techniques such as brainstorming, NGT, affinity diagram, or process mapping to enhance our discussion and decision making?
- Can we make decisions? If not, what prohibits this?
- Can we focus on a problem until a resolution is concluded?
- Do we have the ability to translate decisions into action? If not, why?
- Do we have problems vacillating back and forth between strategic and tactical issues?
- How do we handle disagreement?
- When disagreement occurs, who typically facilitates agreement?

Protocols

Teams should develop and observe protocol in their decision-making processes.

(1) Decisions must be made by all members, not just by a subset. Because some teams are too large, their leader or CEO often relies on a small group within the team to deliberate on issues and make decisions.

As a result, members who are "out" are alienated and hurt and tend to cause conflicts. Conversely, members who are "in" tend to be self-important and arrogant. Although using a small group is a practical alternative to a lengthy all-member deliberation, it can harm team cohesiveness if not coordinated appropriately. All members of the team must be aware of each of their function within the team, especially the roles of the decision-making group.

(2) Decision-making methods must be determined for each issue. Will a vote be taken? If so, will the decision be determined by a majority of the votes? On some decisions, do some members' votes weigh more than others (e.g., is the CEO's vote more significant?)? By discussing their decision-making methods in depth, the team can avoid the Abilene paradox.*

(3) Divergent suggestions or ideas, as long as they don't damage the cohesiveness of the team, must not be discouraged. A member's unique perspectives can actually strengthen decision making because it offers the team creative solutions and innovative ideas.

(4) Organizational position or expertise of any member must not cause imbalance of decisions. Teams have the tendency to allow clinical decisions to be guided solely by the chief nursing officer or the chief medical officer. Although clinical expertise certainly plays a major factor in those types of issues, members without such training can also offer meaningful and creative approaches.

---

*This situation describes a day in which an entire family made a long trip to Abilene simply because one person suggested it and the others believed that everyone wanted to go there. In the end, as the family returned from Abilene and discussed their trip, they discovered that, in reality, none of them had originally wanted to go in the first place.

(5) Proper decorum and courtesy must always be practiced. Respect and honor in debate and deliberation are essential to effective team outcomes.

CONCLUSION

Many teams become so involved in performing their processes that they fail to evaluate if those processes still function in their favor. Each mechanism of a team is unique, just as each part of a vehicle is unique. Overuse it and ignore it, and it is bound to break down. Care for it and restore it, and it is bound to ride with you for a long time.

*   *   *

SELF-EVALUATION QUESTIONS

- What is the make-up of my team? Do we reward others in the organization by asking them to be part of our leadership team?
- Do meetings in our organization make sense? Do others believe this?
- Is my team skilled in decision making? How do I know this?
- Do we have protocols for decision making?

Chapter Seventeen

EVALUATE YOURSELF

This is the single most powerful investment we can ever make in life—investment in ourselves, in the only instrument we have with which to deal with life and to contribute. We are the instruments of our own performance, and to be effective, we need to recognize the importance of taking time regularly to sharpen the saw.

Stephen R. Covey[1]

A T THIS POINT, SOME READERS may have already engaged in self-evaluation, while some may have arrived here without personalizing any of the points given earlier. To those who belong to the former group, I say I am glad that this book encouraged you to reflect on your careers and all of its possibilities and impossibilities. To the latter group, I say please read more; I have more convincing tales to tell.

To ensure that all types of leaders are appropriately addressed in this book, I have provided suggestions for each: early careerists—those who are in the first ten years of their careers; mid careerists—those who have spent the first ten years and looking forward to more; and late careerists—those who are in the final ten years of their careers.

SELF-EVALUATION SUGGESTIONS

FOR ALL CAREERISTS

Write a personal mission statement. A personal mission statement is the roadmap of any careerist. It keeps track of your location—Am I happy, frustrated, or indifferent about my personal life and my career? Is where I am where I want to be? It tells you when you are lost—What did I do to fail? It steers you to the right direction—If I'm satisfied, how can I remain this way? If I'm unhappy, how can I reverse it? Most importantly, it carries you there faster—How did I get here so quickly?

A personal mission statement should articulate the values that guide you to think, to act, and to react to the world around you. It should answer the following questions.

- What is my purpose in life?
- What is my ultimate personal goal?
- What is my ultimate professional goal?
- What do I enjoy doing most?
- How and where do I make the most impact?
- How would I like my obituary to read? (Although morbid, this concept forces you to shape the course of your life.)

Writing a draft for the first time is daunting, taxing, frustrating, and awkward. Constant rewrite eases this tension, however. Completing a statement is a great reward because (1) as you gather your thoughts, you learn more about—and better appreciate—yourself, and (2) you will always have it to monitor your behavior. Some leaders save old statements to compare and contrast with their new one. One executive has a 30-plus-year collection of personal mission statements and personal self-evaluation notes that he peruses and reviews annually to check himself. According to him, this practice helps him find the "true north" of his personal life and career.

Although a personal mission statement should not be shared with anyone else, I will display two as examples (see Figure 17.1).

Take inventory of your personality preferences and leadership style. No matter the tool, you must occasionally evaluate your personal and professional self to track your direction and remain sharp. The Kuder Career Assessment or the Myers-Briggs Type Indicators are among the more popular assessment tools in the market. Although the validity and applicability of these tools may be questionable, they initiate the evaluation process. Perhaps the best tools—and validated ones—available today are the Hogan Personality Inventory; the Hogan Development Survey; and the Hogan Motives, Values and Preferences Inventory. These inventories are more applicable to the skills and styles that workers have today and better reflect the leadership competency systems that many organizations have begun to develop. Several search consultant firms are also beginning to use assessment instruments to assess candidates.

Take inventory of your values. Because your values carry you, you must make sure that they carry you to the right direction. Constant evaluation of your values and how they affect your behavior and thoughts as a person and as a leader ensures that you are on the right track. Team-building retreats is one of the places that provide an opportunity for thought-provoking discussion on values.

FOR EARLY CAREERISTS

Get a mentor. There is much you need to learn about leadership so you must find a seasoned teacher. In my book, *Protocols for Healthcare Executive Behavior*, I argue that effective leaders

FIGURE 17. 1
Sample Personal
Mission Statements

SAMPLE 1

My faith and my family are the most important things in my life. I want to be remembered by my family as a loving spouse and a caring parent. I want my children to remember that I did do an effective job of balancing work and home. I want my spouse to be comfortable with my desire to make a difference in healthcare.

I will end up compromising these values if I take a bigger better job with more prestige. I do not want to do this. Therefore, I must be cautious in being tempted by these kinds of jobs. I will enjoy serving in an organization where I can make a personal impact without neglecting my children and spouse.

Although I want to be a CEO, I understand that the trade off with my family is not worth that price. So, I will try to serve my CEO so effectively that he will include me in more of his decision making, give me greater authority, and I will gain greater fulfillment. This will give me much of the satisfaction typically enjoyed by CEOs.

I will try to work in organizations that respect and support work/family balance. I will try to show this same respect for my division managers.

At the end of my life, I would like to be remembered as a person who was effective in balancing both family and career and one who did not allow work and career to take over.

SAMPLE 2

I entered healthcare to serve others. As a clinician, I studied the art and science of healing. I want to keep this healing mission the central focus of my working life. I want others to know me as a person who always puts patients first. I will be a good steward of the skills given me and will work to get others around me to develop and sustain the passion for patient care that I possess.

I want to work in organizations who put missions first and margin second. I do not want to be affiliated with organizations that are not committed to high quality. I do not want to work in the for-profit health sector.

must have strong skills and knowledge in four areas—technical, administrative, human resources, and protocols.[2] Healthcare administration and management courses often put so much spotlight on the importance of accumulating and honing the first three areas that too little light is shed on the fourth area—protocols, which are societal and organizational expectations about proper behavior and reaction. As a result, many new leaders conduct themselves inappropriately and often leave a poor impression. A mentor can clarify tacit interpersonal concepts like these and provide insight about the inner workings of being a leader.

Always be prepared. Although the question "What are your strengths and weaknesses?" is one of the most anticipated in an interview, many interviewees' responses to it reveal poor preparation. Whether or not the answer to the question helps the candidate is moot, however. What truly matters is that the candidate is prepared because being prepared makes anyone quick, sharp, interested and interesting, and competent—these characteristics are what instantly impress people.

Know your areas of expertise and difficulty. Your awareness of your own abilities and limitations empowers you to control what you can improve and what you can master. Although you feel esteemed that you can communicate well, you must not be complacent and you must seek ways to master your skill. Similarly, although you are humbled by your limitations, you must be practical enough to realize that if you do not enhance your skills your career will perish.

To make his team—and executive candidates—aware of the eight critical competencies that he subscribes to and leaders must possess, one CEO distributes to them the following list.

- Concise communication skills and ability to focus
- Listening skill

- Strategic thinking skills and avoidance of turf orientation
- Consistent purpose and behavior
- Drive and initiative
- Lead by influence not power
- Customer focus
- Goal-oriented and results-driven

The CEO uses this list to guide him in evaluating the performance of all his executives annually. Several of these executives have adopted it and use it their own organizations. Early careerists benefit from this list because it explicitly enumerates expectations.

The Air Force has a simple credo: Integrity first, service before self, and excellence in all that we do. Early careerists should develop their styles and behaviors along these lines.

Broaden your perspective. Many early careerists tend to focus on only one organizational function—strategic planning, financial analysis, operations, human resources, etc. Although this practice accelerates their chance of becoming masters at a certain discipline, it also curbs their creativity and narrows their perspective. Learning to become a leader is tantamount to attending a liberal arts university in that you as a student must study areas beyond your "major" or point of interest to hear voices other than your own, to become familiar with practices other than what you are accustomed to, and to expand your knowledge base and ultimately your reach. Become a generalist during your early years and study all the functions of an organization. Talk, listen, shadow, network, ask, even befriend people who can "show you the ropes." You may not become an expert at all the areas soon—or ever—but at least you understand the mechanics of each function now. In the future you may become a specialist but even then you will still remember the generalist perspective, and the people who have taught you will still remember your avid interest.

Be a keen observer. Early careerists mostly focus on gaining project experience during their tenure. As a result, they are often oblivious to the tacit effects of organizational politics that produces red tape, power struggles, and failed processes. Although formatted as questions, the following are statements that hint at the conflicts within teams.

- What are organizational politics? What is its function within systems and teams?
- What goes on in leadership team meetings?
- How does the CEO prepare the board for decision making?
- When are most organizational decisions made? How are they announced?
- How do senior leaders "sell" their ideas?
- How is conflict suppressed and/or managed?

Be inquisitive. You as an early careerist are expected to ask questions because you are new to the system, you are new to the club, and you are viewed as someone who cannot possibly know very much. Generally, people feel invaluable and charitable when they contribute even a nugget of expertise so take advantage of that good will. Nobody loses in this type of exchange.

Complete your work. Consider each assigned project as a test of your knowledge, your patience, and your potential for success. Invest into it as much time and sweat as is necessary because nothing less than good is expected. Every element of it must be validated, double-checked, and withstand questioning. This means that computational errors and omissions are not acceptable, and that all elements are fully evaluated and must corroborate with given conclusions.

Continue to learn. Education does not stop with the completion of a graduate degree. In fact in the school of leadership, a graduate degree is only an entrance ticket. Once you get inside, a lifelong of formal and informal education and training awaits you. You must take the initiative to pursue these educational opportunities because they do not exist to merely burden you or slow down your pace.

Be prepared for change. As I have been repeating throughout this book, change is inevitable in the healthcare industry so expect it and accept it. The early stage of your leadership career is the optimum moment to consider other career possibilities, especially when the pace or stresses of this responsibility exhausts, terrifies, or displeases you. If you have not experienced any of the pressures yet, you will eventually—just consult Chapter 1. However, I am not trying to instill fear in your heart, I am only warning you that difficult times are ahead and if you are beginning to doubt your career choice now, chances are you may not regain your strong resolve. However, I will not suggest that you leave the industry altogether—not yet at least—because job opportunities that can benefit from your education, training, skills, and experience exist. Talk to seasoned leaders, jot down the pros and cons of your career, consult your personal mission statement, read as much leadership-related literature as you can, and, most importantly, soul search.

Go to job interviews. Some early careerists spend five to six years in their first jobs without considering a move to either another position or another organization. Is this out of loyalty to the organization, department, or position itself? Is this out of fear of rejection—or success? Is this out of aversion to the interview process? Is this out of hope for seniority or promotion? Is this out of love for the job? Whatever the reasons and regardless of how mundane or noble they are, early careerists cannot allow themselves to stagnate or burn out so early. There is absolutely nothing wrong with staying in one place for a long time; in fact many successful leaders retire from the same organizations that originally hired them. However, because the industry today is often in flux it exacts a much different mandate on its leaders. As a result the burn-out factor is higher, especially among new, younger leaders. The remedy then is to utilize techniques, such as interviewing, that help them market their strengths and weaknesses, articulate their future goals, discover their earning and career potentials, learn about the job market, and interact with professionals outside of their regular work setting. Interviews not only sharpen the communication and bargaining skills of early careerists, they also provide them fresh perspective.

SUGGESTIONS FOR MID CAREERISTS

Slow down and take stock. Busy is the most uttered word in the life of a mid careerist. You get pulled by the activities and goings on of your families and friends and you get pulled by your professional responsibilities. With all these different directions, no wonder some mid careerists lack time to evaluate their careers and keep everything in perspective, and no wonder they develop poor interpersonal skills—becoming less personable, less considerate, and more impatient by the minute.

Although slowing down seems incongruent with keeping up with everything, it may just be the panacea for all these ailments. Slow down and write down your answers to the following questions.

- What value system do you follow in your personal life? in your professional life?
- Are you satisfied with what you are doing in your personal life? in your professional life?
- Is your life on track? career?
- Are your accomplishments what you want them to be?

Slow down and re-read your personal mission statement. Compare and contrast it with your answers to the questions above.

Are your answers eerily similar or drastically different? If you display the symptoms above, chances are your answers have dramatically changed. If this is the case, you have serious soul searching ahead and serious career decisions to make. Although career changes are frequent for mid careerists, they can be disruptive particularly in cases when uprooting families is involved.

Reassess your commitment to your values. Early careerists are evaluated more on their *personal leadership attributes and results* while mid careerists are evaluated more on *organizational results*. Because of this evaluation expectation, some mid careerists become so obsessed with producing organizational results that they stop at nothing, including violating ethics. They may distort financial or operating indicators, use their power to hide problems, or point blame to others when it should rest with them.

Unfortunately, these violations are overlooked as long as the organizational results are positive. When this happens, a reexamination of the personal mission statement and renewal of commitment to values are imperative.

Utilize a 360-degree feedback program. Fear is the main reason that mid careerists do not get useful, frank feedback from their subordinates. Because even CEOs need to be evaluated, an anonymous tool completed by a mix of peers and subordinates must be used, such as the 360-degree feedback. Tallying the ratings and comments and properly evaluating them take up significant time so it should be administered only every two to three years.

Continue to network. Because mid careerists often occupy positions that require them to design processes, they always need to refresh and sharpen their creativity. Because networking is a forum in which colleagues can exchange ideas and use each other as sounding boards, it breeds innovative ideas and fresh approaches. Networks also provide you with a group who can — voluntarily or involuntarily — critique your plans, suggest alternatives, and even try your ideas.

Mentor others, especially early careerists. Mentoring someone is beneficial to both parties involved. Being a mentor allows you to be part of shaping someone else's career. If you ever wished that someone told you about the implicit, unwritten, nonverbal rules that are prevalent within your organization, you must become a mentor. If you ever wished that someone were there to discuss and advise you on decisions that turned into your biggest mistakes, then you must become a mentor. If you ever wished that someone who can relate to your experiences were there to celebrate your victories and counsel you in your defeats, then you must become a mentor.

Unfortunately, the higher managers move in an organization, the less likely they are to hear direct, pertinent, and helpful criticism.

Carson Dye[3]

Mentoring also forces you to reevaluate your own career choices because your mentoree will often surprise you with questions that you have never considered. One former CEO admitted that she left her office to return to being a COO after one inquiry from her mentoree; the mentoree asked if she were doing what she liked doing. This question made her realize what she missed, which was running day-to-day operations, and motivated her to return to what was enjoyable for her.

Consider teaching. Mentoring is fundamentally equal to teaching. Teaching, however, is traditionally more structured, abides by rigid schedules, and requires much preparation. Practitioners are valuable additions to the faculty of any graduate program in healthcare administration or management. Practitioners strengthen the credibility of the program in that many students prefer learning from teachers with experience in the industry — teachers who have applied, and possibly have created their own, methodologies that are enumerated in their books or course materials; and those who have actually failed and succeeded at making real-world, organization-wide decisions.

The reward for practitioners is that they remain informed, sharp, and taught. To stay ahead of constant student questions, practitioners must read about current healthcare trends, issues, and concerns. To provide insightful comments when students barrage them with career-choice inquiries, practitioners have to constantly reevaluate their own choices and check their value base. To remain composed when students challenge their thoughts, practitioners must keep an open mind and reflect instead of react. Teaching, as does mentoring, increases the practitioner's ability to relate to others, but most importantly to relate to her/himself.

Continue working with a mentor. This point of your career may be the most momentous because it is at this time that you experience more of the principles you learned earlier. An ongoing relationship with a mentor—if you do not have one, seek one—keeps you on track with the goals you set for yourself because the mentor can help you prioritize. Because your mentor is your senior and over the years becomes a faithful confidant, she/he can also give you free coaching on professional crises such as reorganization or conflict management. Another role for your mentor is as a personal counselor on lifestyle-changing decisions such as relocation, career changes, and career sabbaticals. Many senior-level executives in many industries still retain a mentor, so take heed.

SUGGESTIONS FOR LATE CAREERISTS

Continue to live by your values. If the strength of your values sustained your success you should never let go of them, as one CEO said: "You have made a very good mark in your career. This is not the time to blow it."

Unfortunately, stories about senior executives—not necessarily healthcare executives—who get caught compromising their values to achieve a goal persist, which amplifies the notion that no one in any industry—amateur or expert—is immune to the seductive power of her/his office. Being unethical is easy in many organizations. Late careerists seldom, if ever, receive coaching about many areas in the organization, let alone receive an evaluation about their ethical conduct and the implications of that conduct. Their performance evaluations mostly focus on their ability to increase profitability, market share, and physician satisfaction. Very little attention is given to behavior as long as these numbers are up, which gives late careerists an opportunity to abandon their values and take chances that they would not otherwise take at any other stages in their careers.

Revisit your personal mission statement. Although at this stage of your career—and depending on when you plan to retire—you only have ten or so remaining years to fulfill your professional objectives (but certainly many more years to fulfill your personal goals), you must reread your mission statement. The reason for this is twofold: (1) your mission statement—the same one you wrote at the early or mid stages of your career—reconnects you to the values you live by and the goals you set; and (2) by revisiting it you are reminded not only of your accomplishments but also of your failures and shortcomings. These failures and shortcomings exist to motivate you to continually improve as a person and as a leader.

Prepare for retirement. For active and busy executives, retirement can be traumatic because their everyday pace dramatically slows down; their level of control decreases as they enter a more relaxed non-work setting; and the fear of inactivity settles in. Because retirement is an inevitable event, you must prepare for it. Gradually prepare your staff for the transition by disclosing relevant matters about your responsibilities. Financially prepare yourself and family. The following are preparation methods that actual retired CEOs developed and implemented.

- Develop a personal mission statement for your retirement years.
- Develop a phase-out plan that will move you to a less rigorous, but equally challenging field such as teaching. One CEO taught for nine years at a small local college after retirement.

Avoid skepticism and bitterness. Some late careerists tend to question the commitment and contribution of "today's generation" and become skeptical or cynical about the contributions of those in their organizations. This negativity is counterproductive and petty, and will only make your pre-retirement years burdensome.

Write a tribute to yourself. This is a good time for you to pat yourself on the back for the changes you implemented that revolutionized your organization's processes. Toast yourself for all your positive contributions that still affect people's lives. Make your tribute to yourself another document that comprises the things that people will remember about you.

CONCLUSION

If this book has not convinced you that a leadership imperative exists, adequately defined the true meaning of leadership, or urged you to improve your interaction and skills by continued education and evaluation, then I hope it has at the very least stirred you to examine your values.

All chapters in this book contain self-evaluation questions that allow you to apply the real-world concepts to your real-world scenarios. All examples — actual and fictionalized — in this book focused on the correlation between subscribing to good values and becoming efficient to show that inefficiencies are not a mystery. All three appendices to this book are designed to assess your values—as a person, as a leader, and as a member of a team.

At times, academics and researchers challenge the views harbored by leadership practitioners because the view by the latter group tends to eschew research or hard facts. Conversely, practitioners accuse academics and researchers of relying too much on empirical evidence and not enough on intuitive, practical results. Because I am a practitioner, I was curious to know how my hypotheses fared against the measuring stick of a seasoned leadership researcher. Chapter 18—Measuring Leader Values and Effectiveness— provides the answer. In this chapter, Jared Lock, an industrial psychologist skilled in the area of leadership assessment and development, details the empirical data and literature that support the values-based concepts identified in this book.

The rest of the work is up to you. As Lao Tzu says, there is much to be done, so good luck.

> Great organizations invariably decline. Great monuments eventually decay. Great accomplishments are always surpassed. All that is achieved invites its own eclipse. As long as life continues, there is more to be or do.

> Lao Tzu[4]

* * *

SELF-EVALUATION QUESTIONS

- Have I ever formally, verbally or in writing, evaluated my leadership successes and/or failures?
- Have I written a personal mission statement?

- Have I taken any formalized leadership assessment tools or inventories? Have I applied what they taught me to improving my leadership style and skills?
- How do I want to be remembered?
- Do I take (make) ample time for my career? Do I engage in any type of planning related to it?

Chapter Eighteen

MEASURING LEADER VALUES AND EFFECTIVENESS

by Jared D. Lock, Ph.D.
Hogan Assessment Systems

...the field of leadership is presently in a state of ferment and confusion. Most of the theories are beset with conceptual weaknesses and lack strong empirical support.... The confused state...can be attributed in large part to the disparity of approaches, the narrow focus of most researchers, and the absence of broad theories to integrate findings from the different approaches.

Yukl and Van Fleet[1]

I HAVE TO ADMIT THAT I am usually very skeptical when reading leadership books and believe that most are the accumulation of subjective ideas with no real data to support the "conclusions." This book asserts in great part that reconnecting leaders to their values will increase leader effectiveness, which in turn will lead to improved healthcare organizations. Although this book uses popular literature to identify its points, it does not identify the empirical research that in fact does support this conceptualization. Examples include:

- Employees' goals are the most important contributor to how the team organizes itself and how they will react to the organization.[2]
- Team members are highly sensitive to how their leader responds to the organization's vision and values.[3]
- How a leader responds to the organization's vision and values is related to the leader's own personal characteristics, managerial derailment tendencies, and values.[4]
- Team members adjust their actions and goals to reflect their leader's response to the organization's vision and values.[5]
- Team effectiveness is directly related to the degree to which the team's goals and the organization's goals are similar. This is true even when the leader is trying to change the organization because lower performance (at least initially) is a common outcome of the change process.[6]

A review of the academic literature does support the fact that a leader's values are related to effectiveness, as indicated throughout this book. Moreover, it also indicates that organizations should spend time identifying how job behaviors of leaders facilitate, hinder, or do not agree with the organization's mission, vision, and value statements. The literature also indicates that measures of normal personality, managerial derailment characteristics, and values can be used to assess the leader's dispositions.

MEASURING LEADER VALUES

Given the empirical linkage between leader values and effectiveness, organizations would want to consider how these values might be measured. Prior to using any values-based assessment, though, organizations should determine if the assessment (a) measures values and (b) is related to job performance.

DOES THE ASSESSMENT MEASURE VALUES?

When reviewing the values mentioned in the previous chapters, these values actually describe combinations of three separate, yet related, personality domains: normal personality, managerial derailment characteristics, and values. Each of these is discussed below.

Normal Personality. Normal personality helps an organization describe what *positive* actions are associated with a leader's values. Normal personality includes characteristics that describe a person's usual way of interacting with others. The Five-Factor Model of Personality, which is based on 50 years of factor analytic research,[7] indicates that a person's reputation (i.e., personality) can be defined in terms of five dimensions:[8]

(1) Emotional Stability (Adjustment)
(2) Ascendance (Sociability and Ambition)
(3) Agreeableness (Likeability)
(4) Conscientiousness (Prudence)
(5) Openness (Intellect and Continuous Learning)

Wiggins (1979) found that most common personality measures can be described in terms of these five dimensions, and as such has become the industry standard for assessments.[9]

Managerial Derailment Characteristics. "Managerial derailment" (defined as the failure of a seemingly able leader) focuses not on the characteristics that make a good leader, but on those negative characteristics that hinder performance.

> There is an understandable tendency to attribute monstrous deeds accompanied by callousness, remorselessness, lying, and failure to accept responsibility to a monstrous nature. This attributional tendency leaves one in mute

incomprehension of how ordinary people, as well as re-spected leaders, can coldly perpetrate atrocities—as they regularly do—under a variety of circumstances and incentives.[10]

Poor managerial performance is a widespread problem. One out of every two managers is not performing up to expected levels.[11] Leaders who are derailing often also have good social skills and apparent leadership potential. This makes these dysfunctional characteristics difficult to measure in an employment interview. And, unfortunately, there are a limited number of well-validated measures of derailment characteristics. Managerial derailment characteristics can be used to describe the *negative* actions that are associated with leader's values. The Hogan Development Survey (HDS) measures overextension (i.e., to the point of performance problems) of the following characteristics:[12]

- Excessive emotionality
- Paranoia
- Lack of self-confidence
- Poor social judgment
- Procrastination
- Arrogance
- Deceitfulness
- Self-dramatizing tendencies
- Bad judgment and poor influence skills
- Perfectionistic tendencies
- Dependent tendencies

Values. The final personality domain explicitly concerns values—those characteristics that can be used to explain *why* a person manifests the personal characteristics described above. Values are often confused with needs and interests. Values, needs, and interests are highly interrelated[13]; the main difference is in abstraction, with interests being the least abstract and values being the most abstract.

We have had good success measuring values with the Motives, Values, Preferences Inventory (MVPI),[14] a 10-scale inventory designed to evaluate the fit between an individual and the organization's values. It assesses values at multiple levels and under different circumstances. These scales include the main concepts behind the motive, attitude, value, need, interest, goal, and commitment theories espoused over the past 80 years.[15] These ten values include:

(1) Art, culture, and project quality
(2) Belonging; establishing relationships; getting along with others
(3) Helping others; customer orientation
(4) Making money; concern with organizational finances
(5) Having fun; being open to others
(6) Being influential; wanting to be in charge
(7) Valuing data-based problem solving; technologically interested
(8) Valuing playing it safe; resistant to change
(9) Valuing conservative over liberal management style
(10) Valuing tradition, ritual, history, and old-fashioned values

DOES THE ASSESSMENT PREDICT LEADER EFFECTIVENESS?

The second question concerns an assessment's relationship with job performance. Leader values affect organizations in three major areas: employment selection, individual development, and team development, which are all associated with job performance. Any value measure should be valid. Validity is simply the ability to predict non-test outcomes like job performance. Although this seems straightforward, many common assessments actually ignore validity. For instance, even though there is no evidence that it predicts job performance or leader effectiveness,[16] many consultants and organizations incorrectly use the Myers-Briggs Type Indicator for selection decisions.

SUMMARY

Although there are numerous assessments available, few actually measure values as described in this book (e.g., *why* people perform the way they do). If properly measured, values can be a rich source of leader effectiveness data. Most values and personality measures, however, lack validity evidence; test publishers owe it to organizations to show how their assessments are job related.

MEASURING LEADER EFFECTIVENESS

Although most organizations consider financial performance the number one indicator of leader effectiveness (and it is important to track financial variables), focusing solely on financial outcome will do little to improve leadership. This is mainly because financial results do not identify *what the leader did, why the leader did it,* or *what the leader could have done better.* Also, many uncontrollable forces (e.g., market, legislation, seasonal fluctuations, luck, huge layoffs for short-term gains, etc.) affect financial outcome. Thus, we recommend focusing on what the leader does and this leads to two questions. What should be measured? How should we interpret these measures?

What should be measured? This is easily answered by referring to the following quote: "[One of the worst problems in industry is] the failure of executives to advance the interests of their companies."[17] Our definition of leadership (the ability to get others to put aside their own self-interests, for a while, in order to pursue the interests of the team) reflects both (a) motivation in general and (b) specific motivation toward a common goal. Good leaders will not simply motivate their employees, but motivate them toward goals that lead to desired organizational outcomes. The importance of measuring a team's drive toward an organization's goals can be summarized as follows:

- Team counterproductivity is linked to a discrepancy between the leader's and the organization's goals.[18]
- Over time, an organization takes on the personality characteristics—both positive and negative—of those who lead it.[19]
- Leaders control which goals are identified as important during goal development, goal verbalization, and subordinate acceptance.[20]

Leaders' impression on their team's goals and values comes from the interaction between their own and their organizations' goals and values.[21] In practice, organizations should spend time studying the goals, mission, vision, and values to identify those leader behaviors that are conducive to success. Once the behaviors are identified, measures can be created to track the performance levels of leaders in this regard.

How should we interpret these measures? Measuring adherence and performance to organizational goals does not tell us how to interpret results. The relevant research can be summarized as follows:

- Most leader and team effectiveness research has deemed the work team or team as the best level of analysis with respect to gauging a leader's effectiveness.[22]

- Many employees have trouble understanding or visualizing the linkage between their work behaviors and desired organizational outcomes and look to their leaders because they think they will actually direct them in ways that are consistent with the vision.[23]
- Leader values have been found to affect team performance.[24]
- Organizational values that are similar to those of their leaders will tend to be more heavily emphasized by those leaders.[25]

This summary suggests that work teams understand those organizational values that are linked to the leader's values and their behaviors will reflect this association. Therefore, when evaluating leader effectiveness, organizations should note (a) the similarity between a team's actions and the organization's mission, goals, vision, and values and (b) the degree to which team members work toward the same mission, vision, and values.

SUMMARY OF THE EMPIRICAL RESEARCH

This section summarizes what we know about leader values and effectiveness. When possible, the titles and names used in the book chapters will be used to increase understanding. The research can be summarized in five points.

(1) **There is a common core of leader values that improves performance.** The following values are associated with success in virtually every leader position.

- Ethics and Integrity[26]
- Relationship Orientation[27]
- Desire to Make a Difference and Commitment[28]
- Emotional Intelligence[29]
- Trustworthiness[30]

- Cooperation and Sharing. These are important to the extent that quality is maintained.[31]
- Team Conflict. How the leader responds to the team conflict is an important aspect of judging leader success.[32] Leaders are judged as less effective if they are seen as "know-it-alls" who are unwilling to listen to others. Leaders will be judged as more effective if they welcome team conflict as a way of unifying divergent thought processes. As always, the leader's effectiveness in dealing with a team conflict should take into consideration how the end results converge with the organization's goals, mission, vision, and values.

(2) **Leaders often fail because of negative values.** Most discussions of leadership usually focus on positive characteristics that can positively affect job performance. There is a growing body of research, however, that indicates leadership flaws are just as important to leader effectiveness. This can explain the difference between "natural-born leaders" and leaders who have to work harder to get the same results. Leaders with similar personalities, interpersonal skills, and abilities can, and often do, differ in their performance. Although flawed leadership would seem to be a low base-rate phenomenon, in a study of hospital leaders,[33] the empirical evidence suggests that the base rate of leader incompetence is between 50 percent and 60 percent. In other words, more than half of all healthcare leaders are causing employee stress and company failure.

Why is this important? Sarbin (1954) found that people with good social skills appear to possess different qualities than they actually do (i.e., are good liars) and others have found that this correlates with perceived performance.[34] As cited by Goleman (1990), Hogan states "superior self-presentation skills drive careers, not competence. Someone with a narcissistic personality disorder, for instance, is motivated to succeed because of an unhealthy craving for attention and recognition, not out of a desire to do a good job."[35] This research indicates potential problems when selecting leaders.

Most healthcare organizations are accustomed to using executive search firms to identify leadership candidates. In addition, most healthcare organizations still rely on the interview, with no systematic assessment of candidate's characteristics and values. Finally, of those organizations that do use assessments, few if any actually use a measure of dysfunctional characteristics to identify potential performance flaws.

(3) **Healthcare organizations should be focusing rather intently on managerial derailment.** Our research has concluded that:

- The managerial derailment characteristics are rarely detected in interviews.[36]
- The managerial derailment characteristics are negatively correlated with leader performance.[37]
- The managerial derailment characteristics are negatively correlated with agreement among team members on the team's mission and values.[38]
- Arrogance, passive-aggression, and untrustworthiness are the main managerial derailment characteristics that are not adequately assessed during an interview.
- Poor hiring decisions are associated with huge expenditures to remove or develop the leader.

(4) **Leaders should have common values, but different interests.** Although this may make intuitive sense, leaders with similar values tend to get along better and have fewer disagreements. On the other hand, leaders with similar values tend to want to perform the same activities, concentrate on the same agenda items, and overlook other aspects of the organization.[39] To be successful, all leadership teams should include individuals with interests that emphasize operations, finance, marketing, human resources, leadership, and management. A lack of attention to any one of these areas could lead to decreased decision-making quality.

(5) **Leader values affect the bottom lines of organizations.** With respect to leader's values, the following simple argument can be made from all of the research presented in this chapter. First, employees look to their leaders to determine what is important in the workplace and how they should respond. Second, the values of leaders in organizations directly impact the way they translate organizational mission, vision, values, and goals to their teams. Third, similarity between team actions and organizational vision will lead to goal attainment. Finally, organizational outcomes will lead to improved operations and service to patients and others.

CONCLUSION

I conclude this chapter with a summary and encourage the reader to (a) question the veracity of statements made in leadership books and (b) to read the citations for more clarity. I conclude with the following four points.

(1) **Leader values are important determinants of individual, team, and organization success.** The values of leaders impact their ability to influence organizational outcomes, rally support for organizational initiatives, make positive decisions, and also help determine the job satisfaction and success of those leaders. Leader values should be consistent with those of their organizations and leaders should freely express these values.

(2) **Leader values can and should be assessed with well-validated assessments that have a documented history of predicting performance outcomes.** Although the test-publishing business is a growing industry, not all assessments are developed equally. Any assessment that is used to describe leader values or performance should be based on data showing that it predicts job performance. Values are part of the larger context of personality assessment and concern the internal motivations that contribute to job behaviors.

(3) **Assessments should be used in conjunction with interviews as an objective evaluation of a person's potential fit with the job and the organization.** Any assessment used as part of the selection system should have a well-established linkage with successful job performance. A "gut feeling" gained from a set of interviews is just not enough, given the sophistication of healthcare leaders and the interview training received.

(4) **Leader values are statistically correlated with their effect on the organization's bottom line.** This is a particularly salient reason to take seriously the

advice offered in this book. Most healthcare organizations are greatly challenged today in ensuring that operations are run effectively, and the fact that the bottom line is constantly scrutinized means that organizations should take every step possible to maximize stakeholder value. Understanding leader values and their potential impact in organizations is a simple and reliable way to maximize your human resources.

NOTES

1. Yukl and Van Fleet 1992
2. Cattell 1946; Hogan, Curphy, and Hogan 1994; Hogan, DeSoto, and Solano 1977; McDougal 1908
3. Pollak and Weiner 1995
4. Lock 1996, 1998; Lock and Thomas 1999
5. Doyle 1992; Guzzo and Shea 1992; Litwin and Stringer 1968; Manz and Sims 1987
6. Meglino, Ravlin, and Adkins 1989; Stumpf and Hartman 1984
7. Digman 1990; Goldberg 1992, 1993; Hogan 1992; McCrae and Costa 1987
8. Hogan 1992
9. Wiggins 1979
10. Levenson, Kiehl, and Fitzpatrick 1995
11. Shipper and Wilson 1991
12. Hogan and Hogan 1997
13. Hogan and Blake 1996
14. Hogan and Hogan 1996
15. Hogan and Hogan 1996
16. Myers, et al. 1998
17. R. Hogan as quoted by Goleman 1990
18. Hackman 1987; O'Brien and Harary 1977
19. Kets de Vries and Miller 1986

20. Kouzes and Posner 1987
21. Borman and Motowidlo 1993; Cattell 1946; Doyle 1992; Guzzo and Shea 1992; Hogan, Curphy, and Hogan 1994; Hogan, DeSoto, and Solano 1977; Litwin and Stringer 1968; Manz and Sims 1987; McClelland and Burnham 1976; McDougal 1908; Meglino, Ravlin, and Adkins 1989; Pollak and Weiner 1995; Stumpf and Hartman 1984
22. Campion, Medsker, and Higgs 1995; Golden 1992
23. Klimoski and Jones 1995
24. George 1990; Hackman 1987; Hollander 1985; Hollander and Offerman 1990; Jackson 1991; Parker 1990
25. Lock and Thomas 1998
26. Bentz 1990; McClelland and Burnham 1976; Yukl and Van Fleet 1992
27. Bentz 1985; Conger and Kanungo 1990; Hogan 1994; House 1977
28. Bass 1990; Batkins 1982; Bentz 1990; Browning and Jacob 1964; Conger and Kanungo 1990; Cummin 1967; Hill 1976; Hoffman and Hoffman 1970; Hogan 1994; House 1977; McClelland and Burnham 1976; O'Brien and Harary 1977; Shaw and Harkey 1976; Stahl 1983; Veroff 1957; Wainer and Rubin 1969; Yukl and Van Fleet 1992
29. Conger and Kanungo 1990; Hogan 1994; House 1977; McClelland and Burnham 1976; Yukl and Van Fleet 1992
30. Bass 1990; Bentz 1985; Berube 1982; Hackman 1987; Hallam and Campbell 1992; Harris and Hogan 1992; Hogan and Lock 1995; Hogan, Curphy, and Hogan 1994; Hogan and Hogan 1994; Kouzes and Posner 1987; Lock 1996, 1997; Lombardo, Ruderman, and McCauley 1988; Lorr, Youniss, and Stefic 1991; McCall and Lombardo 1983; O'Brien and Harary

1977; Redding 1972; Sgro, Worchel, Pence, and Orban 1980

31. Hogan 1994; McClelland and Burnham 1976
32. Ghiselli 1963; Hogan and Hogan 1992
33. Shipper and Wilson 1991
34. Mowday 1978
35. Goleman 1990
36. Hogan and Hogan 1997
37. Hogan and Hogan 1994
38. Lock 1997
39. Holland 1985

Appendix A

EVALUATE YOUR EMOTIONAL INTELLIGENCE

DIRECTIONS: EMOTIONAL INTELLIGENCE is a person's maturity quotient. Maturity is the ability to manage emotions, make sound decisions, positively influence others, and possess strong self-awareness. The questions below were selected to assess the emotional intelligence of a person in the workplace based on the perception of those she/he works, or worked, directly with.

Read each question carefully and circle the selection that most appropriately describes the person being evaluated. Although there are no right or wrong answers, you are encouraged to reflect on each question and answer as accurately as possible.

You have been asked to evaluate _____ along several interpersonal dimensions. Five or more individuals—peers and subordinates—are completing this questionnaire. When you are finished, please return your questionnaire to _____, who will compile the results and provide summary averages to the person named above. Because the questionnaire does not require your name, your responses are anonymous; please do not share your responses with anyone.

What is your relationship to the person being evaluated? Please check one.

____ Peer (work at same organization)
____ Peer (work elsewhere)
____ Subordinate
____ Superior (full-time paid boss)
____ Superior (voluntary board member)
____ Other

1. This leader creates the feeling that he/she looks forward to each day with positive anticipation.

Strongly Disagree	Disagree	Neither Disagree or Agree	Agree	Strongly Agree
1	2	3	4	5

2. This leader truly believes that her/his work really makes a difference in her/his organization.

Strongly Disagree	Disagree	Neither Disagree or Agree	Agree	Strongly Agree
1	2	3	4	5

3. This leader is a person with an even temper.

Strongly Disagree	Disagree	Neither Disagree or Agree	Agree	Strongly Agree
1	2	3	4	5

4. This leader rarely gets frustrated.

Strongly Disagree	Disagree	Neither Disagree or Agree	Agree	Strongly Agree
1	2	3	4	5

5. This leader has the creative ability to solve problems among people.

Strongly Disagree	Disagree	Neither Disagree or Agree	Agree	Strongly Agree
1	2	3	4	5

6. This leader truly enjoys being with other people.

Strongly Disagree	Disagree	Neither Disagree or Agree	Agree	Strongly Agree
1	2	3	4	5

7. This leader has strong control of her/his emotions.

Strongly Disagree	Disagree	Neither Disagree or Agree	Agree	Strongly Agree
1	2	3	4	5

8. When times get tough in the work setting, others can turn to this leader for guidance.

Strongly Disagree	Disagree	Neither Disagree or Agree	Agree	Strongly Agree
1	2	3	4	5

9. When mistakes are made, this leader's first instinct is to take corrective action (rather than place blame).

Strongly Disagree	Disagree	Neither Disagree or Agree	Agree	Strongly Agree
1	2	3	4	5

10. Other people would describe this leader as a person who does not "fall apart" under pressure.

Strongly Disagree	Disagree	Neither Disagree or Agree	Agree	Strongly Agree
1	2	3	4	5

11. This leader is well suited for her/his career.

Strongly Disagree	Disagree	Neither Disagree or Agree	Agree	Strongly Agree
1	2	3	4	5

12. If this leader had the chance to start her/his career all over again, she/he would still choose a leadership position.

Strongly Disagree	Disagree	Neither Disagree or Agree	Agree	Strongly Agree
1	2	3	4	5

13. This leader respects other people.

Strongly Disagree	Disagree	Neither Disagree or Agree	Agree	Strongly Agree
1	2	3	4	5

14. This leader is highly motivated.

Strongly Disagree	Disagree	Neither Disagree or Agree	Agree	Strongly Agree
1	2	3	4	5

15. Others would say this leader has her/his ego under control.

Strongly Disagree	Disagree	Neither Disagree or Agree	Agree	Strongly Agree
1	2	3	4	5

16. This leader has an appropriately high level of self-esteem.

Strongly Disagree	Disagree	Neither Disagree or Agree	Agree	Strongly Agree
1	2	3	4	5

17. Although this leader may at times get upset or angry, she/he has the ability to control these emotions.

Strongly Disagree	Disagree	Neither Disagree or Agree	Agree	Strongly Agree
1	2	3	4	5

18. This leader has an appropriately high level of motivation.

Strongly Disagree	Disagree	Neither Disagree or Agree	Agree	Strongly Agree
1	2	3	4	5

19. This leader always seeks win-win solutions in situations of conflict.

Strongly Disagree	Disagree	Neither Disagree or Agree	Agree	Strongly Agree
1	2	3	4	5

20. This leader would be the last person I would describe as a hopeless individual.

Strongly Disagree	Disagree	Neither Disagree or Agree	Agree	Strongly Agree
1	2	3	4	5

21. Although impatient for positive results, this leader does not allow her/his impatience to create a negative working environment.

Strongly Disagree	Disagree	Neither Disagree or Agree	Agree	Strongly Agree
1	2	3	4	5

22. This leader is a person whom others trust.

Strongly Disagree	Disagree	Neither Disagree or Agree	Agree	Strongly Agree
1	2	3	4	5

23. This leader is appropriately self-confident without being overbearing.

Strongly Disagree	Disagree	Neither Disagree or Agree	Agree	Strongly Agree
1	2	3	4	5

24. This leader is sensitive to the feelings of others.

Strongly Disagree	Disagree	Neither Disagree or Agree	Agree	Strongly Agree
1	2	3	4	5

25. This leader listens well.

Strongly Disagree	Disagree	Neither Disagree or Agree	Agree	Strongly Agree
1	2	3	4	5

26. The last description you would expect to hear of this individual is: "She/He flies off the handle a lot."

Strongly Disagree	Disagree	Neither Disagree or Agree	Agree	Strongly Agree
1	2	3	4	5

27. This leader maintains a good balance in life.

Strongly Disagree	Disagree	Neither Disagree or Agree	Agree	Strongly Agree
1	2	3	4	5

28. This leader is emotionally very stable and healthy.

Strongly Disagree	Disagree	Neither Disagree or Agree	Agree	Strongly Agree
1	2	3	4	5

29. This leader faces setbacks and adversity well.

Strongly Disagree	Disagree	Neither Disagree or Agree	Agree	Strongly Agree
1	2	3	4	5

30. This leader would *not* be described as hostile.

Strongly Disagree	Disagree	Neither Disagree or Agree	Agree	Strongly Agree
1	2	3	4	5

31. This leader has developed good mechanisms to get feedback from others.

Strongly Disagree	Disagree	Neither Disagree or Agree	Agree	Strongly Agree
1	2	3	4	5

Appendix B

EVALUATE EACH COMPONENT
OF YOUR LEADERSHIP TEAM

ALTHOUGH THIS QUESTIONNAIRE has not been validated (i.e., no study has been performed to determine the correlation between the results of this questionnaire and performance outcome—such as profitability, patient satisfaction, physician satisfaction, and employee satisfaction), it provides the team an initial tool with which to assess each of the components that contributes to its effectiveness.

Because each component contributes to the overall efficiencies and inefficiencies of the team, each must be independently evaluated. Below is a categorized list of each of these components. To ensure comprehensive representation, all team members must complete the questionnaire. To ensure confidentiality of the responses, the team must select a neutral third party to collect the questionnaires, tally the ratings, and write a report, which will be distributed to the team for discussion.

Directions: Rate the following questions as correctly as possible. Please submit your completed questionnaire to (name of third party) by (date). Please do not share your responses with others.

TEAM LEADERSHIP

1.   The CEO or leader is not autocratic.

Not at All	To a Small Extent	Some-what	To a Great Extent	Totally and Com-pletely
0	3	5	7	10

2.   The CEO or leader does not make team decisions outside meetings. The CEO or leader develops an atmosphere that encourages openness.

Not at All	To a Small Extent	Some-what	To a Great Extent	Totally and Com-pletely
0	3	5	7	10

3.   The CEO or leader is not afraid to be a full and equal participant in team processes.

Not at All	To a Small Extent	Some-what	To a Great Extent	Totally and Com-pletely
0	3	5	7	10

4. In establishing the team, the CEO or leader ensures that all team members understand the decisions that should be made within the team setting and the decisions that should be made outside the team setting.

Not at All	To a Small Extent	Some-what	To a Great Extent	Totally and Com-pletely
0	3	5	7	10

5. The CEO or leader ensures that time is set aside to occasionally discuss roles and decision-making rules and protocols.

Not at All	To a Small Extent	Some-what	To a Great Extent	Totally and Com-pletely
0	3	5	7	10

TEAM COMPATIBILITY

6. Members come from common backgrounds.

Not at All	To a Small Extent	Some-what	To a Great Extent	Totally and Com-pletely
0	3	5	7	10

7.   Members have personal compatibility.

Not at All	To a Small Extent	Some-what	To a Great Extent	Totally and Com-pletely
0	3	5	7	10

8.   Members have professional compatibility.

Not at All	To a Small Extent	Some-what	To a Great Extent	Totally and Com-pletely
0	3	5	7	10

TEAM INTERACTION

9.   Members have camaraderie.

Not at All	To a Small Extent	Some-what	To a Great Extent	Totally and Com-pletely
0	3	5	7	10

10.   Members occasionally socialize outside of the workplace.

Not at All	To a Small Extent	Some-what	To a Great Extent	Totally and Com-pletely
0	3	5	7	10

11. The team has frequent communication.

Not at All	To a Small Extent	Some-what	To a Great Extent	Totally and Com-pletely
0	3	5	7	10

12. The team has open and candid conversations.

Not at All	To a Small Extent	Some-what	To a Great Extent	Totally and Com-pletely
0	3	5	7	10

13. The team has accurate discussions and limits exaggeration and information hiding.

Not at All	To a Small Extent	Some-what	To a Great Extent	Totally and Com-pletely
0	3	5	7	10

TEAM MINDSET AND STRUCTURE

14. Members are committed to the same goals.

Not at All	To a Small Extent	Some-what	To a Great Extent	Totally and Com-pletely
0	3	5	7	10

15. All members understand their roles within the team.

Not at All	To a Small Extent	Some-what	To a Great Extent	Totally and Com-pletely
0	3	5	7	10

16. Members have actively and openly discussed their roles.

Not at All	To a Small Extent	Some-what	To a Great Extent	Totally and Com-pletely
0	3	5	7	10

17. Members have mutually agreed to the assignment of these roles.

Not at All	To a Small Extent	Some-what	To a Great Extent	Totally and Com-pletely
0	3	5	7	10

18. Members are highly interdependent on one another.

Not at All	To a Small Extent	Some-what	To a Great Extent	Totally and Com-pletely
0	3	5	7	10

19. The team has a high energy level.

Not at All	To a Small Extent	Some-what	To a Great Extent	Totally and Com-pletely
0	3	5	7	10

20. Conflict is acknowledged, discussed, and managed by all members.

Not at All	To a Small Extent	Some-what	To a Great Extent	Totally and Com-pletely
0	3	5	7	10

21. Members are very frank with each other and engage in very little politics.

Not at All	To a Small Extent	Some-what	To a Great Extent	Totally and Com-pletely
0	3	5	7	10

22. The size of the team is between four and twelve.

Not at All	To a Small Extent	Some-what	To a Great Extent	Totally and Com-pletely
0	3	5	7	10

23. There is a proper balance of titles among members.

Not at All	To a Small Extent	Some-what	To a Great Extent	Totally and Com-pletely
0	3	5	7	10

TEAM MEETINGS

24. Meetings are well organized.

Not at All	To a Small Extent	Some-what	To a Great Extent	Totally and Com-pletely
0	3	5	7	10

25. Meetings have objectives.

Not at All	To a Small Extent	Some-what	To a Great Extent	Totally and Com-pletely
0	3	5	7	10

26. The agenda is followed closely during meetings.

Not at All	To a Small Extent	Some-what	To a Great Extent	Totally and Com-pletely
0	3	5	7	10

27. Team members show appropriate courtesy to each other during meetings.

Not at All	To a Small Extent	Some- what	To a Great Extent	Totally and Com- pletely
0	3	5	7	10

28. All team members actively participate in meetings.

Not at All	To a Small Extent	Some- what	To a Great Extent	Totally and Com- pletely
0	3	5	7	10

29. Meetings have an appropriate level of formality but are not stiff.

Not at All	To a Small Extent	Some- what	To a Great Extent	Totally and Com- pletely
0	3	5	7	10

30. Meetings are ended with an understood conclusion.

Not at All	To a Small Extent	Some- what	To a Great Extent	Totally and Com- pletely
0	3	5	7	10

TEAM DECISIONS

31. The team observes decision-making protocols.

Not at All	To a Small Extent	Some- what	To a Great Extent	Totally and Com- pletely
0	3	5	7	10

32. The entire team is responsible for decision making.

Not at All	To a Small Extent	Some- what	To a Great Extent	Totally and Com- pletely
0	3	5	7	10

33. The entire team has been trained in decision-making techniques.

Not at All	To a Small Extent	Some- what	To a Great Extent	Totally and Com- pletely
0	3	5	7	10

34. The team has openly discussed their decision-making styles and processes.

Not at All	To a Small Extent	Some- what	To a Great Extent	Totally and Com- pletely
0	3	5	7	10

35. The entire team realizes the danger of utilizing compromise as the only end-result in a decision-making process.

Not at All	To a Small Extent	Some-what	To a Great Extent	Totally and Com-pletely
0	3	5	7	10

Appendix C

EVALUATE YOUR PROFESSIONAL
AND PERSONAL VALUES

OUR VALUES REVEAL US MORE CLEARLY through our behavior than through our words. Civility often prevents us from saying what we mean, but it does not always prevent us from reacting with our body. As a result, we give out two varying reactions to one scenario.

This questionnaire assesses your values based on your perception and others' perception. It contains two tools—self-perception and others' perception.

Directions: After you complete the self-perception questionnaire, ask two to three of your fellow team members, whom you think know you well, to complete the others' perception questionnaire. Ideally you will want to have them give their completed questionnaires to a neutral third party to compile averages and ranges for the answers. Doing this will increase the honesty of others when evaluating you. Following discussions with the neutral third party, you may then want to meet with the individuals who evaluated you to compare and contrast all perceptions.

SELF-PERCEPTION OF VALUES

1. To what extent do you respect other people?

Not at All	To a Small Extent	Some-what	To a Great Extent	Totally and Com-pletely
0	3	5	7	10

2. To what extent do you serve as a good steward of the talent, authority, resources, and position you hold?

Not at All	To a Small Extent	Some-what	To a Great Extent	Totally and Com-pletely
0	3	5	7	10

3. To what extent are you an ethical person?

Not at All	To a Small Extent	Some-what	To a Great Extent	Totally and Com-pletely
0	3	5	7	10

4. To what extent do you keep your word?

Not at All	To a Small Extent	Some-what	To a Great Extent	Totally and Com-pletely
0	3	5	7	10

5. To what extent do you seek to develop positive and wholesome relationship with others?

Not at All	To a Small Extent	Some- what	To a Great Extent	Totally and Com- pletely
0	3	5	7	10

6. To what extent do you desire to serve others?

Not at All	To a Small Extent	Some- what	To a Great Extent	Totally and Com- pletely
0	3	5	7	10

7. To what extent do you desire to make a difference and effect positive change and contributions?

Not at All	To a Small Extent	Some- what	To a Great Extent	Totally and Com- pletely
0	3	5	7	10

8. To what extent are you committed to the vision and goals of your organization?

Not at All	To a Small Extent	Some- what	To a Great Extent	Totally and Com- pletely
0	3	5	7	10

9. To what extent do you work hard?

Not at All	To a Small Extent	Some-what	To a Great Extent	Totally and Com-pletely
0	3	5	7	10

10. To what extent are you a highly dedicated person?

Not at All	To a Small Extent	Some-what	To a Great Extent	Totally and Com-pletely
0	3	5	7	10

11. To what extent are you emotionally mature?

Not at All	To a Small Extent	Some-what	To a Great Extent	Totally and Com-pletely
0	3	5	7	10

12. To what extent do you value the contributions of a team?

Not at All	To a Small Extent	Some-what	To a Great Extent	Totally and Com-pletely
0	3	5	7	10

13. To what extent do you cooperate with fellow team members?

Not at All	To a Small Extent	Some-what	To a Great Extent	Totally and Com-pletely
0	3	5	7	10

14. To what extent do you share information and other resources with fellow team members?

Not at All	To a Small Extent	Some-what	To a Great Extent	Totally and Com-pletely
0	3	5	7	10

15. To what extent do you try to build trust with others?

Not at All	To a Small Extent	Some-what	To a Great Extent	Totally and Com-pletely
0	3	5	7	10

16. To what extent are you willing to trust others?

Not at All	To a Small Extent	Some-what	To a Great Extent	Totally and Com-pletely
0	3	5	7	10

17. To what extent do you affirmatively try to bring conflict to the surface to manage it effectively?

Not at All	To a Small Extent	Some- what	To a Great Extent	Totally and Com- pletely
0	3	5	7	10

OTHERS' PERCEPTION OF _____ VALUES

(insert name here)

1. To what extent does your colleague respect other people?

Not at All	To a Small Extent	Some- what	To a Great Extent	Totally and Com- pletely
0	3	5	7	10

2. To what extent does your colleague serve as a good steward of the talent, authority, resources, and position she/he holds?

Not at All	To a Small Extent	Some- what	To a Great Extent	Totally and Com- pletely
0	3	5	7	10

3. To what extent is your colleague an ethical person?

Not at All	To a Small Extent	Some- what	To a Great Extent	Totally and Com- pletely
0	3	5	7	10

4. To what extent can your colleague keep her/his word?

Not at All	To a Small Extent	Some-what	To a Great Extent	Totally and Com-pletely
0	3	5	7	10

5. To what extent does your colleague seek to develop positive and wholesome relationship with others?

Not at All	To a Small Extent	Some-what	To a Great Extent	Totally and Com-pletely
0	3	5	7	10

6. To what extent does your colleague desire to serve others?

Not a All	To a Small Extent	Some-what	To a Great Extent	Totally and Com-pletely
0	3	5	7	10

7. To what extent does your colleague desire to make a difference and effect positive change and contributions?

Not a All	To a Small Extent	Some-what	To a Great Extent	Totally and Com-pletely
0	3	5	7	10

8. To what extent is your colleague committed to the vision and goals of your organization?

Not at All	To a Small Extent	Some-what	To a Great Extent	Totally and Com-pletely
0	3	5	7	10

9. To what extent does your colleague work hard?

Not at All	To a Small Extent	Some-what	To a Great Extent	Totally and Com-pletely
0	3	5	7	10

10. To what extent is your colleague a highly dedicated person?

Not a All	To a Small Extent	Some-what	To a Great Extent	Totally and Com-pletely
0	3	5	7	10

11. To what extent is your colleague emotionally mature?

Not a All	To a Small Extent	Some-what	To a Great Extent	Totally and Com-pletely
0	3	5	7	10

12. To what extent does your colleague value the contributions of a team?

Not at All	To a Small Extent	Some-what	To a Great Extent	Totally and Com-pletely
0	3	5	7	10

13. To what extent does your colleague cooperate with fellow team members?

Not at All	To a Small Extent	Some-what	To a Great Extent	Totally and Com-pletely
0	3	5	7	10

14. To what extent does your colleague share information and other resources with fellow team members?

Not a All	To a Small Extent	Some-what	To a Great Extent	Totally and Com-pletely
0	3	5	7	10

15. To what extent does your colleague try to build trust with others?

Not a All	To a Small Extent	Some-what	To a Great Extent	Totally and Com-pletely
0	3	5	7	10

16. To what extent is your colleague willing to trust others?

Not at All	To a Small Extent	Some-what	To a Great Extent	Totally and Com-pletely
0	3	5	7	10

17. To what extent does your colleague affirmatively try to bring conflict to the surface to manage it effectively?

Not at All	To a Small Extent	Some-what	To a Great Extent	Totally and Com-pletely
0	3	5	7	10

Sources

PREFACE

1. Kouzes, J. M., and B. Z. Posner. 1987. *The Leadership Challenge.* San Francisco: Jossey-Bass Publishers.

CHAPTER 1

1. Kotter, J. P. 1996. *Leading Change.* Boston: Harvard Business School Press.
2. Mintzberg, H. 1998. "Covert Leadership: Notes on Managing Professionals." *Harvard Business Review* (November–December): 140.
3. Halvorson, G. C. 1993. *Strong Medicine.* New York: Random House.
4. Drucker, P. 1997. Quoted in "Getting Beyond Industrial Logic: Renewing Our Faith in the Value of Health," by Shari Mycek. *Healthcare Forum Journal* 40 (4): 16–20.

5. Pfeffer, J. 1998. *The Human Equation: Building Profits by Putting People First.* Boston: Harvard Business School Press.

6. Sherman, V. C. 1993. *Creating the New American Hospital.* San Francisco: Jossey-Bass Publishers.

7. Beckham, J. D. 1999. "The Crash of ValuJet 592: Implications for Healthcare." *Health Forum Journal* 42 (1).

8. Olson, M. I., L. Werner Carr, D. P. Bourque, et al. 1999. 1999 *Environmental Assessment: Rising to the Challenge of a New Century.* Irving, TX: VHA Inc., and Deloitte & Touche LLP.

9. Shortell, S. M. (ed.) 1996. *Remaking Health Care in America.* San Francisco: Jossey-Bass Publishers.

10. Adams, S. 1996. *The Dilbert Principle: A Cubicle's-Eye View of Bosses, Meetings, Management Fads and Other Workplace Afflictions.* New York: HarperBusiness.

CHAPTER 2

1. Kreitner, R., and A. Kinicki. 1998. *Organizational Behavior, Fourth Edition.* New York: Richard D. Irwin.

2. Kotter, J. A. 1990. *A Force for Change: How Leadership Differs from Management.* New York: The Free Press.

3. Stogdill, R. 1984. *Stogdill's Handbook of Leadership: A Survey of Theory and Research.* New York: The Free Press.

4. Kreitner, R., and A. Kinicki. 1997. *Organizational Behavior, Fourth Edition.* New York: Richard D. Irwin.

5. Hughes, R. L., R. C. Ginnett, and G. J. Curphy. 1998. *Leadership: Enhancing the Lesson of Experience,*

Third Edition. New York: Richard D. Irwin.

6.   *Ibid.*

7.   Robbins, S. P. 1999. *Essentials of Organizational Behavior.* Upper Saddle River, NJ: Prentice Hall.

8.   Covey, S. R. 1990. *The Seven Habits of Highly Effective People: Powerful Lessons in Personal Change.* New York: Fireside Press.

CHAPTER 3

1.   Goldsmith, J. 1998. "Three Predictable Crises in the Health System and What to Do About Them." *Healthcare Forum Journal* November–December.

CHAPTER 4

1.   Kushner, H. S. 1986. *When All You've Ever Wanted Isn't Enough.* New York: Summit Books.

2.   Block, P. 1993. *Stewardship: Choosing Service Over Self-interest.* San Francisco: Berrett-Koehler Publishers.

3.   Hargrove, R. 1998. *Mastering the Art of Creative Collaboration.* New York: McGraw-Hill.

4.   Dye, C. 1993. *Protocols for Healthcare Executive Behavior.* Chicago: Health Administration Press.

5.   Kaplan, R. 1991. *Beyond Ambition: How Driven Managers Can Lead Better and Live Better.* San Francisco: Jossey-Bass Publishers.

6.   Williams, M. 1975. *The Classic Tale of the Velveteen Rabbit.* New York: Avon Books.

CHAPTER 5

1.   Merry, M. D. 1996. "Physician Leadership: The Time Is Now!" *Physician Executive* 22 (9).

2. Branden, N. 1998. "The Psychology of Self-Esteem." In *Heart at Work* by J. Canfield and J. Miller. New York: McGraw-Hill.

3. Burns, J. M. 1978. *Leadership*. New York: Harper and Row.

4. Merriam Webster. 1995. *Merriam Webster's Collegiate Dictionary, Tenth Edition*. Springfield, MA: Merriam-Webster, Inc.

5. Cooper, R. K., and A. Sawaf. 1997. *Executive EQ: Emotional Intelligence in Leadership and Organizations*. New York: Perigee Books – The Berkley Publishing Co.

6. Hughes, R. L., R. C. Ginnett, and G. J. Curphy. 1998. *Leadership: Enhancing the Lesson of Experience, Third Edition*. New York: Richard D. Irwin.

CHAPTER 6

1. Covey, S. R. 1990. *Principle-Centered Leadership*. New York: Fireside Press.

2. Kouzes, J. M., and B. Z. Posner. 1993. *Credibility: How Leaders Gain and Lose It, Why People Demand It*. San Francisco: Jossey-Bass Publishers.

3. Benton, D. A. 1992. *Lions Don't Need to Roar: Using the Leadership Power of Professional Presence to Stand Out, Fit in and Move Ahead*. New York: Warner Books.

4. Scholtes, P. R. 1998. *The Leader's Handbook: Making Things Happen, Getting Things Done*. New York: McGraw-Hill.

5. Bennis, W., and R. Townsend. 1997. *Reinventing Leadership: Strategies to Empower the Organization*. New York: William Morrow and Co.

6. *Ibid.*

7. Kouzes, J. M., and B. Z. Posner. 1993. *Credibility: How Leaders Gain and Lose It, Why People Demand It.* San Francisco: Jossey-Bass Publishers.

CHAPTER 7

1. Greenleaf, R. K. 1983. *Servant Leadership: A Journey into the Nature of Legitimate Power and Greatness.* Mahwah, NJ: The Paulist Press.
2. *Ibid.*
3. Conger, J. 1989. *The Charismatic Leader: Behind the Mystic of Exceptional Leadership.* San Francisco: Jossey-Bass Publishers.

CHAPTER 8

1. Isomura, I. 1998. In *Organizational Behavior, Fourth Edition* by R. Kreitner and A. Kinicki. New York: Richard D. Irwin.
2. McClelland, D. C. 1961. *The Achieving Society.* New York: Free Press.
3. Kaplan, R. S., and D. P. Norton. 1996. *The Balanced Scorecard.* Boston: Harvard Business School Press.
4. MacStravic, S. C. 1999. "A Really Balanced Scorecard." *Health Forum Journal* May–June.
5. Kouzes, J. M., and B. Z. Posner. 1993. *Credibility: How Leaders Gain and Lose It, Why People Demand It.* San Francisco: Jossey-Bass Publishers.
6. Peters, T. 1987. *Thriving on Chaos: Handbook for a Management Revolution.* New York: Alfred A. Knopf.
7. Smith, D. K. 1996. *Taking Charge of Change: 10 Principles for Managing People and Performance.* New York: Addison-Wesley.

8. Conger, J. 1989. *The Charismatic Leader: Behind the Mystic of Exceptional Leadership.* San Francisco: Jossey-Bass Publishers.

CHAPTER 9

1. Engstrom, T. W., and E. R. Dayton. 1984. *The Christian Leader's 60-Second Management Guide.* Waco, TX: Word Books.
2. Ross, A. 1992. *Cornerstones of Leadership for Health Services Executives.* Chicago: Health Administration Press.
3. Maxwell, J. C. 1998. *The 21 Irrefutable Laws of Leadership: Follow Them and People Will Follow You.* Nashville, TN: Thomas Nelson Publishers.
4. Covey, S. R. 1990. *The Seven Habits of Highly Effective People: Powerful Lessons in Personal Change.* New York: Fireside Press.
5. Katzenbach, J. R., and D. K. Smith. 1993. *The Wisdom of Teams.* Boston: Harvard Business School Press.

CHAPTER 10

1. Drucker, P. 1997. Quoted in "Getting Beyond Industrial Logic: Renewing Our Faith in the Value of Health," by Shari Mycek. *Healthcare Forum Journal* 40 (4): 16–20.
2. Weisinger, H. 1998. *Emotional Intelligence at Work: The Untapped Edge for Success.* San Francisco: Jossey-Bass Publishers.
3. Goleman, D. 1998. *Working with Emotional Intelligence.* New York: Bantam Books.
4. Weisinger, H. 1998. *Emotional Intelligence at Work: The Untapped Edge for Success.* San Francisco:

Jossey-Bass Publishers.
5. *Ibid.*

CHAPTER 11

1. Covey, S. R. 1990. *Principle-Centered Leadership.*
New York: Fireside Press.
2. McKinsey & Company. 1998. "The War for Talent"
(study). *Search Connection* 16: 2.
3. Katzenbach, J. R., and D. K. Smith. 1993. *The
Wisdom of Teams.* Boston: Harvard Business School
Press.
4. Adapted from *Touchstones: Ten New Ideas
Revolutionizing Business* by W. A. Band. 1994. In
Organizational Behavior, Fourth Edition by R.
Kreitner and A. Kinicki. 1998. New York: Richard
D. Irwin.

CHAPTER 12

1. Hughes, R. L., R. C. Ginnett, and G. J. Curphy.
1998. *Leadership: Enhancing the Lesson of
Experience, Third Edition.* New York: Richard D.
Irwin.

CHAPTER 13

1. Scholtes, P. R. 1998. *The Leader's Handbook:
Making Things Happen, Getting Things Done.* New
York: McGraw-Hill.
2. Merriam Webster. 1995. *Merriam Webster's
Collegiate Dictionary, Tenth Edition.* Springfield,
MA: Merriam-Webster, Inc.
3. Kouzes, J. M., and B. Z. Posner. 1987. *The Leadership
Challenge.* San Francisco: Jossey-Bass Publishers.

4. Maurer, R. 1996. *Beyond the Wall of Resistance: Unconventional Strategies That Build Support for Change.* Austin, TX: Bard Press.
5. Kotter, J. A. 1996. *Leading Change.* Boston: Harvard Business School Press.
6. Robbins, S. P. 1999. *Essentials of Organizational Behavior.* Upper Saddle River, NJ: Prentice Hall.

CHAPTER 14

1. Zalesnik, A. 1997. "Real Work." *Harvard Business Review* (November–December): 60.
2. Eisenhardt, K. M., J. L. Kahwajy, and L. J. Bourgeois, III. 1997. "How Management Teams Can Have a Good Fight." *Harvard Business Review* (July–August): 77.
3. Smith, D. K. 1996. *Taking Charge of Change: 10 Principles for Managing People and Performance.* New York: Addison-Wesley.
4. Kreitner, R., and A. Kinicki. 1998. *Organizational Behavior, Fourth Edition.* New York: Richard D. Irwin.

CHAPTER 15

1. Katzenbach, J. R., and D. K. Smith. 1993. *The Wisdom of Teams.* Boston: Harvard Business School Press.
2. Kimball, L., and A. Eunice. 1999. "Virtual Team: Strategies to Optimize Performance." *Health Forum Journal* 42 (4): 59.

CHAPTER 16

1. Scholtes, P. R. 1998. *The Leader's Handbook: Making Things Happen, Getting Things Done.* New

York: McGraw-Hill.
2.   Robbins, S. P. 1999. *Essentials of Organizational Behavior.* Upper Saddle River, NJ: Prentice Hall.

CHAPTER 17

1.   Covey, S. R. 1990. *The Seven Habits of Highly Effective People: Powerful Lessons in Personal Change.* New York: Fireside Press.
2.   Dye, C. 1993. *Protocols for Healthcare Executive Behavior.* Chicago: Health Administration Press.
3.   *Ibid.*
4.   Herman, S. M., and Lao-Tzu Tao Te Ching. 1994. *The Tao at Work: On Leading and Following.* San Francisco: Jossey-Bass Publishers.

CHAPTER 18

Bass, B. 1990. *Bass and Stogdill's Handbook of Leadership: Theory, Research, and Applications, Third Edition.* New York: Free Press.

Batkins, J. 1982. "A Descriptive Study of Power...." *Dissertation Abstracts International* 43 (2B): 505.

Bentz, J. 1985. A View from the Top.... Paper presented at the annual meeting of the American Psychological Association, Los Angeles, California.

Bentz, J. 1990. "Contextual Issues in Predicting High-level Leadership Performance...." In *Measures of Leadership* by K. Clark and M. Clark (eds.), 131–43. West Orange, NJ: Leadership Library of America.

Berube, M. (ed.). 1982. *The American Heritage Dictionary,*

Second Edition. Boston: Houghton Mifflin.

Borman, W., and S. Motowidlo. 1993. "Expanding the Criterion Domain...." In *Personnel Selection in Organizations* by N. Schmitt, W. Borman, and Associates (eds.). San Francisco: Jossey-Bass Publishers.

Browning, R., and H. Jacob. 1964. "Power Motivation and Political Personality." *Public Opinion Quarterly* 28: 75–90.

Campion, M., G. Medsker, and A. Higgs. 1993. "Relations Between Work Group Characteristics...." *Personnel Psychology* 46: 823–50.

Cattell, R. 1946. *Description and Measurement of Personality.* Yonkers-on-Hudson, NY: World Book.

Conger, J., and R. Kanungo. 1990. A Behavioral Attribute Measure.... Paper presented at the annual meeting of the Academy of Management, San Francisco, California.

Cummin, P. 1967. "TAT Correlates of Executive Performance." *Journal of Applied Psychology* 51: 78–81.

Digman, J. 1990. "Personality Structure...." *Annual Review of Psychology* 41: 417–40. Palo Alto, CA: Annual Reviews.

Doyle. 1992. "Caution: Self-directed Work Teams." *HR Magazine* (June): 153–54.

George, J. M. 1990. "Personality, Affect, and Behavior in Groups." *Journal of Applied Psychology* 75 (2): 107–16.

Ghiselli, E. 1963. "Intelligence and Managerial Success."

Psychological Reports 12: 898.

Goldberg, L. 1992. "The Development of Markers of the Big-Five Structure." *Psychological Assessment* 4: 26–42.

Goldberg, L. 1993. "The Structure of Phenotypic Personality Traits." *American Psychologist* 48: 26–34.

Golden, K. 1992. "The Individual and Organizational Culture...." *Journal of Management Studies* 29 (1): 1–21.

Goleman, D. 1990. "The Dark Side of Charisma." *The New York Times*, 1 April, Section 3, Part 2.

Guzzo, R., and G. Shea. 1992. "Group Performance and Intergroup Relations." In *Handbook of Industrial and Organizational Psychology Volume 3, Second Edition* by M. Dunnette and L. Hough (eds.), 269–313. Palo Alto, CA: Consulting Psychologists Press.

Hackman, J. 1987. "The Design of Work Teams." In *Handbook of Organizational Behavior* by J. Lorsch (ed.), 315–41. Englewood Cliffs, NJ: Prentice-Hall.

Hallam, G., and D. Campbell. 1992. Selecting Team Members?.... Paper presented at the annual meeting of the Society of Industrial and Organizational Psychology, Montreal, Quebec, Canada.

Harris, G., and J. Hogan. 1992. Perceptions and Personality Correlates.... Paper presented at the 13th Annual Psychology in the Department of Defense symposium, Colorado Springs, Colorado.

Hill, N. 1976. "Self-esteem: The Key to Effective Leadership."

Administrative Management 31 (8): 24.

Hoffman, S., and I. Hoffman. 1970. "The Will to Grandeur...." In *Philosophers and Kings: Studies in Leadership* by D. Rustow (ed.). New York: George Braziller.

Hogan, J., and R. Hogan. 1996. *Motives, Values, Preferences Inventory Manual.* Tulsa, OK: Hogan Assessment Systems.

Hogan, J., and J. Lock. 1995. A Taxonomy of Interpersonal Skills.... Paper presented in Beyond Technical Requirements for Job Performance symposium at the conference of the Society for Industrial and Organizational Psychology, Inc., Orlando, Florida.

Hogan, R. 1992. "Personality and Personality Measurement." In *Handbook of Industrial and Organizational Psychology Volume 2, Second Edition* by D. Dunnette and L. Hough (eds.), 873–919. Palo Alto, CA: Consulting Psychologists Press.

Hogan, R. 1994. "Trouble at the Top." *Consulting Psychology Journal* 46 (1): 9–15.

Hogan, R., and R. Blake. 1996. "Vocational Interests...." In *Behavior in Organizations* by K. Murphy (ed.), 89–114. San Francisco: Jossey-Bass Publishers.

Hogan, R., G. Curphy, and J. Hogan. 1994. "What We Know About Leadership...." *American Psychologist* 49 (6): 493–504.

Hogan, R., C. DeSoto, and C. Solano. 1977. "Traits, Tests, and Personality Research." *American Psychologist* 32 (4): 255–64.

Hogan, R., and J. Hogan. 1992. *The Hogan Personality Inventory.* Tulsa, OK: Hogan Assessment Systems.

Hogan, R., and J. Hogan. 1994. "The Mask of Integrity." In *Citizen Espionage: Studies in Trust and Betrayal* by T. Sarbin, R. Carney, and C. Eoyang (eds.). Westport, CT: Praeger.

Hogan, R., and J. Hogan. 1997. *The Hogan Development Survey.* Tulsa, OK: Hogan Assessment Systems.

Holland, J. 1985. *Making Vocational Choices: A Theory of Vocational Personalities and Work Environments, Second Edition.* Englewood Cliffs, NJ: Prentice-Hall.

Hollander, E. 1985. "Leadership and Power." In *The Handbook of Social Psychology, Third Edition* by G. Lindzey and E. Aronson (eds.), 485–537. New York: Random House.

Hollander, E., and L. Offerman. 1990. "Relational Factors of Organizational Leadership and Followership." In *Measures of Leadership* by K. Clark and M. Clark (eds.), 83–97. West Orange, NJ: Leadership Library of America.

House, R. 1977. "A 1976 Theory of Charismatic Leadership." In *Leadership: The Cutting Edge* by J. Hunt and L. Larson (eds.). Carbondale: Southern Illinois University Press.

Jackson, S. E. 1991. "Consequences of Group Composition...." In *Advances in Strategic Management, Volume 8* by P. Shrivastava, A. Huff, and J. Dutton (eds.), 345–82. Greenwich, CT: JAI Press.

Kets de Vries, M., and D. Miller. 1986. "Personality, Culture, and Organization." *Academy of Management Review* 11: 266–79.

Klimoski, R., and R. G. Jones. 1995. "Staffing for Effective Group Decision Making...." In *Team Effectiveness and*

Decision Making in Organizations by R. A. Guzzo and E. Salas (eds.), 291–332. San Francisco: Jossey-Bass Publishers.

Kouzes, J., and B. Posner. 1987. *The Leadership Challenge: How to Get Extraordinary Things Done in Organizations.* San Francisco: Jossey-Bass Publishers.

Levenson, M., K. Kiehl, and C. Fitzpatrick. 1995. "Assessing Psychopathic Attributes…." *Journal of Personality and Social Psychology* 68 (1): 151–58.

Litwin, G., and R. Stringer. 1968. *Motivation and Organizational Climate.* Boston: Harvard University, Graduate School of Business.

Lock, J. 1997. The Relationship Between Trust and Leader–Group Processes. Paper presented in Personality Applications in the Workplace: Thinking Outside the Dots symposium at the twelfth annual conference of the Society for Industrial and Organizational Psychology, St. Louis, Missouri.

Lock, J. 1996. Developing an integrative model of leadership. Unpublished doctoral dissertation. University of Tulsa, Tulsa, Oklahoma.

Lock, J., and L. Thomas. 1998. The Effects of Leader's Values on Group Citizenship. Poster presented at the thirteenth annual conference of the Society for Industrial and Organizational Psychology, Dallas, Texas.

Lombardo, M., M. Ruderman, and C. McCauley. 1988. "Explanations of Success and Derailment in Upper-level Management Positions." *Journal of Business and Psychology* 2: 199–216.

Lorr, M., R. Youniss, and R. Stefic. 1991. "An Inventory of Social Skills." *Journal of Personality Assessment* 57 (3): 506–20.

Manz, C., and H. Sims. 1987. "Leading Workers to Lead Themselves...." *Administrative Sciences Quarterly* 32: 106–28.

McCall, M., and M. Lombardo. 1983. "Off the Track: Why and How Successful Executives Get Derailed" (Tech. Rep. No. 21). Greensboro, NC: Center for Creative Leadership.

McClelland, D., and D. Burnham. 1976. "Power Is the Great Motivator." *Harvard Business Review,* 100–10.

McCrae, R., and P. Costa. 1987. "Validation of the Five Factor Model of Personality Across Instruments and Observers." *Journal of Personality and Social Psychology* 52: 81–90.

McDougal, W. 1908. *Social Psychology.* London: Methuen.

Meglino, B., E. Ravlin, and C. Adkins. 1989. "A Work Values Approach...." *Journal of Applied Psychology* 74: 424–32.

Mowday, R. 1978. "The Exercise of Upward Influence in Organizations." *Administrative Science Quarterly* 23: 137–56.

Myers, I., M. McCaulley, N. Quenk, and A. Hammer. 1998. *Myers-Briggs Type Indicator Manual, Third Edition.* Palo Alto, CA: Consulting Psychologists Press.

O'Brien, G., and F. Harary. 1977. "Measurement of the Interactive Effects of Leadership Style...." *Australian Journal of Psychology* 29: 59–71.

Parker, G. M. 1990. *Team Players and Teamwork: The New Competitive Business Strategy*. San Francisco: Jossey-Bass Publishers.

Pollak, R., and S. Weiner. 1995. Team Assessment System: Factors of Team Effectiveness. Poster session presented at the conference of the Society for Industrial and Organizational Psychology, Inc., Orlando, Florida.

Redding, W. 1972. *Communication with the Organization: An Interpretive Review of Theory and Research*. New York: Industrial Communication Council.

Sarbin, T. 1954. "Role Theory." In *Handbook of Social Psychology* by G. Lindzey (ed.). Reading, MA: Addison-Wesley.

Sgro, J., P. Worchel, E. Pence, and J. Orban. 1980. "Perceived Leader Behavior...." *Academy of Management Journal* 23: 161–65.

Shaw, M., and B. Harkey. 1976. "Some Effects of Congruency of Member Characteristics...." *Journal of Personality and Social Psychology* 34 (3): 412–18.

Shipper, F., and C. Wilson. 1991. The Impact of Managerial Behaviors on Goup Performance, Stress, and Commitment. Paper presented at The Research Conference on Leadership, Center for Creative Leadership, Colorado Springs, Colorado.

Stahl, M. 1983. "Achievement, Power, and Managerial Motivation...." *Personnel Psychology* 36: 775–89.

Stumpf, S., and K. Hartman. 1984. "Individual Exploration to

Organizational Commitment or Withdrawal." *Academy of Management Journal* 27: 308–29.

Veroff, J. 1957. "Development and Validation of a Projective Measure of Power Motivation." *Journal of Abnormal and Social Psychology* 54: 1–8.

Wainer, H., and I. Rubin. 1969. "Motivation of Research and Development Entrepreneurs...." *Journal of Applied Psychology* 53 (3):178–84.

Wiggins, J. 1979. "A Psychological Taxonomy of Trait-Descriptive Terms...." *Journal of Personality and Social Psychology* 37 (3): 395–412.

Yukl, G., and D. Van Fleet. 1992. "Theory and Research on Leadership in Organizations." In *Handbook of Industrial and Organizational Psychology Volume 3, Second Edition* by M. Dunnette and L. Hough (eds.), 147–97. Palo Alto, CA: Consulting Psychologists Press.

About the Author

CARSON F. DYE, FACHE, is a healthcare management and executive search consultant. He conducts chief executive officer, senior executive, and physician executive searches for various healthcare organizations. His consulting experience includes strategic planning, organizational design, and physician leadership. He assists boards in executive and physician compensation, conducts board retreats, and provides counsel in chief executive officers' employment contracts and evaluation matters for a variety of client organizations. He is certified to use the Hogan Assessment Systems tools in executive selection, development, and coaching.

Prior to entering executive search, Mr. Dye was a principal and director of Findley Davies, Inc.'s Health Care Industry Consulting Division. Prior to his consulting career, he served as Chief Human Resources Officer at St. Vincent Medical Center, Ohio State University Medical Center, and Children's Hospital Medical Center.

Mr. Dye has been named as a physician leadership consultant expert on the LaRoche National Consultant Panel and is a member of the Governance Institute Governance One Hundred. He works with Dick Rand as a special advisor to The Healthcare Roundtable.

Mr. Dye teaches physician leadership and organizational behavior courses at Ohio State University. Since 1989, he has taught several programs for the American College of Healthcare Executives and he frequently speaks for state and local hospital associations. He has also authored *Protocols for Health Care Executive Behavior* (1993) and has written several journal articles on leadership and human resources.

Mr. Dye has had a lifelong interest in leadership and its impact on organizations. He has studied how values drive leadership and how they affect change management. In addition, he studies group and organizational structure and its impact on strategy and organizational success.

Mr. Dye earned his BA from Marietta College and his MBA from Xavier University.